ENGLISH EVERYDAY

ENGLISH EVERYDAY
HIGHER-LEVEL ABILITY AND UNDERSTANDING.
LEVEL 1 - THE VERBS

DAVID HERRICK

ENGLISH EVERYDAY
HIGHER-LEVEL ABILITY AND UNDERSTANDING. LEVEL 1 - THE VERBS

iUniverse books may be ordered through booksellers or by contacting:

iUniverse
1663 Liberty Drive
Bloomington, IN 47403
www.iuniverse.com
1-800-Authors (1-800-288-4677)

ISBN: 978-1-5320-4036-8 (sc)
ISBN: 978-1-5320-4035-1 (e)

Library of Congress Control Number: 2018900067

Print information available on the last page.

iUniverse rev. date: 04/11/2018

ENGLISH EVERYDAY - THE VERBS *is a study course for everyone that wants to improve pronunciation and learn new vocabulary.*

Each verb in the book has clear examples of how it is used and pronounced, with an emphasis guide to show you how to say the words correctly.

Whether you are learning English as a second language, or you are improving the skills that you already have, English Everyday can help you become more confident. Your ability to speak English can help you reach your goals in business, education, travel, and meeting new friends.

Your new communication skills will help you understand, and other people will understand you!

HOW TO USE THIS BOOK

English Everyday is an American English curriculum. If you have learned British English, you will see that some words are not spelled the way that you have seen them spelled before. When you listen to the videos on **EnglishEveryday.info**, words are spoken with an American pronunciation.

In English Everyday, pronunciation is the most important focus, and the first two sections will help you understand that English is not always spoken as the written words appear. Because the sounds can be difficult to master, we have created the videos on **EnglishEveryday.info,** and the **English Everyday** channel on YouTube, that go together with the lessons in this book. The words are spoken clearly as you read them on the screen. As you are learning, speak the words and practice pronunciation. Soon, you will be able to make the same sounds and emphasis as the information in the videos.

Many sections of the book are grouped as categories, or families, of verbs, and their corresponding nouns. Categories of similar words are important to learn, because English is a complex language. You will learn the differences and similarities between these similar words, and which words to use for clear communication.

English Everyday

Higher Level Ability and Understanding

TABLE OF CONTENTS

The first step in this program is looking at the correct pronunciation of past-tense verbs. A very common error for many learners is pronouncing all the letters in a word. Past-tense verbs are easy to say incorrectly, because "ed" looks like "ed"!

Ending sounds for past-tense verbs.

Most verbs in the present-tense form are easy to read and pronounce correctly, but when we change the verb to past tense, a 't' or a 'd' sound is used in place of the 'ed' sound.

One example is the verb '**walk**'. The past tense is '**walked**', which sounds like **wokt**. The past tense of the verb '**cook**' is '**cooked**'. When you see the spelling, it is easy to pronounce the word "**cook-ed**", with two syllables.

The *correct* way to say the word is **cookt**, and the pronunciation will be shown this way. [cookt]

Pronunciation guides are in *brackets*, which look like this. []
The words in brackets are *NOT* the correct way to spell the words! It is only for the pronunciation and emphasis.

'**look**' is '**looked**' [lookt], '**rub**' is '**rubbed**' [rubd], and '**clean**' is '**cleaned**' [kleend].
The ending sound is a quick '**t**', like [lookt] or '**d**', like [rubd].

This rule is for verbs that *DO NOT* end with the letter 't' or the letter 'd'.

A verb that ends with the letter 'T' sounds like "____**ted**" when it is used in the past-tense.
A few examples are:
shouted, departed, sorted, started, visited, wanted, invited, deposited, edited.

A verb that ends with the letter 'D' sounds like "____**ded**" when it is used in the past-tense.

A few examples are:
ended, commanded, decided, handed, persuaded, pretended, responded, needed.

Some verbs that end in 'T' do not follow the usual form in the past-tense usage.
'write' is **'wrote'**, **'light'** is **'lit'**, the past tense of **'hit'** is **'hit'**, but the past tense of **'sit'** is **'sat'**!

Some verbs that end in 'D' do not follow the usual form in the past-tense usage.
'bend' is **'bent'**, **'send'** is **'sent'**, **'build'** is **'built'**, **'ride'** is **'rode'**, and **'spend'** is **'spent'**.

Verbs that do not end with –ed for past tense are called **irregular verbs**. There are about 100 verbs in English that are irregular verbs. The most commonly used irregular verb is the verb **"to be"**, and it is VERY irregular, even in present tense! I am, she is, he is, it is, they are, we are, you are.
The future tense is easier. I will be, she will be, we will be, they will be.
But, the past tense is not always easy. I was, she was, we were, they were.

Emphasis, or "Stress", in spoken English.

The emphasis (or *stress*) in a word with two or more syllables is a VERY important part of speaking English. In this book, we have given you written hints about using emphasis when you are saying multi-syllable words (The prefix *"multi"* means more than one).

Example - multiple = more than one thing.
The correct emphasis is on the first syllable - "**MUL**-tih-pull"
If the emphasis changes to the second or third syllable, the word can become difficult to understand or recognize. If you say "mul-**TIH**-pull" or "mul-tih-**PULL**", your message might not be clear.

Because written English does not have clues about where the emphasis in words should be, the only way to learn is to **listen, remember,** and **practice**.

For the correct emphasis, look at the words in the brackets!

*We are confident that you will benefit from the **English Everyday** program, and we are happy to help YOU reach your goals. Are you ready to start?*

Verbs for doing things with our body.

All of these actions can be done by people, and some of the movements can be done by animals, plants, or things that are *not* alive.
Some of the actions are **voluntary** movements = *trying to do, or intending to do, something.* Other actions are **involuntary** movements = *we don't try to do these things. Our body does them automatically. We don't think about it. It just happens, like your heart beating, and breathing the air. Some action verbs can be both voluntary and involuntary.*

Each verb will have up to three different examples, using different verb tenses. If the word can be used as a noun, there is also an example. Sometimes, the word changes form when used as a noun, and the emphasis (stress) might change too. *Pay attention to the examples!*

Verbs for communicating with words.

whisper [WHIS-per] = *speak very quietly without using voice, only air.*
"When I tell a secret, I always whisper." - *present perfect tense*
"She whispered [WHIS-perd] to her friend." - *past-tense verb*
"Those girls are whispering to each other."
"That man heard your whisper." - *noun*

murmur [MER-mer] = *words are spoken quietly, using voice sounds.*
"I did not hear his murmur clearly, but I understood his message. It was time to leave."
"She murmured [MER-merd] something about her boyfriend."

"If he keeps murmuring, I will never understand what he is saying!"
"My father talks when he sleeps. I know what he is dreaming from his murmurs." - *noun*

mumble [MUM-bul] = *words are not spoken clearly, or spoken too quietly to be understood.*
"When you mumble, I cannot understand your words."
"You mumbled [MUM-buld] something that I did not hear clearly."
"I wish you would stop mumbling."
"Your mumbles are difficult to understand!" - *plural noun*

Words and phrases that mean 'murmur' and 'mumble' are: **grumble, speak under your breath, speaking to yourself.**

utter [UH-ter] = *make sounds or words. similar to 'speak', but 'utter' can be used to criticize or insult someone. Not a common word!*
"He will always utter something stupid when he speaks to the teacher."
"Yesterday he uttered [UH-terd] about cows for an hour."
"Today he is uttering about goats."
"What will tomorrow's utterance be?" - *noun*

babble [BAB-bel] = *speaking words clearly and quickly. But, the message is not clear, or not interesting for other people.*
"She likes to babble about her cats all day long."
"His uncle babbled [BAB-beld] on and on about his holiday in France."
"He was babbling something about his dinner wasn't warm and there were no potatoes."
"She can be so boring when she talks, and it is all just tedious babble!" - noun

Words and phrases that mean 'babble' are: **jabber, run on and on about, yack, rattle on, ramble, yammer, chatter.**

yell = *say words very loudly.*
"Please don't yell. I am standing very close to you."
"She yelled [yeld] so loudly that all of her neighbors heard her."
"I wish she would stop yelling."

"Her yell was heard by everyone." - *noun*

shout = *say words very loudly.*

"If somebody is too far away, I have to shout to them."

"I shouted [SHOU-ted] many times, but he could not hear me."

"If I continue shouting, I can get her attention."

"She finally heard my last shout." - *noun*

scream [skreem] = *say words very loudly, at a very high pitch.*

"The teacher will scream at the students when she is angry."

"When the teacher screamed [skreemd], everyone payed attention."

"The teacher is still screaming."

"Her screams are so loud!" - *plural noun*

*Exercise: Choose three different verbs from this group, and make three sentences. Use one (or more) of the following pronouns: **he, she, it, we, they, our, I, you, my, his, her.***

Verbs that use our hands.

hold = *have something in your hand(s).*

"Please hold this bag while I open the door."

"She held a small cat in her hands." - *past-tense verb changes form*

"Are you holding anything in your hand?"

"I lost my hold of the coffee cup, and it fell down." - *noun*

grab = *using your hand(s) to quickly capture something.*

"Quickly! Grab my dog before it runs away!"

"The policeman grabbed [grabd] the thief before he could escape."

"My friend is always grabbing my pencil away from me."

"His quick grab saved the chair from falling." - *noun*

snatch = *using your hand(s) to quickly capture something, or take something away.*

"Be careful, my daughter will snatch your food!"

"He snatched [snatcht] the keys from my hand."
"The thief was snatching a diamond ring when the clerk saw him."
"He grabbed the dragonfly with a quick snatch." - *noun*

touch [tutch] = *using your sense of touch to feel the texture, or other characteristics, of something. We usually touch with our hands, but any part of the body can touch.*
"If you touch the ice, you can feel how cold it is."
"When I touched [tutcht] her hair, it felt like silk."
"The girl is touching the dog's nose with her foot."
"The nurse had a very gentle touch." - *noun*

feel = *using your sense of touch, or a response to a stimulus with any part of your body. Feel can be outside or inside your body. It can also be an emotion.*
"I can feel the heat from the coffee cup."
"He felt something wet inside the bag." - *past-tense verb changes form*
"She is feeling the temperature of the water."
"Mud has a very slippery feel." - *noun*

throw = *make something go through the air by using your hand(s) and arm(s).*
"The boy wants to throw his food on the floor."
"She threw the ball to her friend." - *past-tense verb changes form*
"They are throwing rocks at a bottle."
"That was a really good throw!" - *noun*

catch [katch] = *to capture something that is moving with your hand(s).*
"We will catch a lot of frogs today."
"He caught [kawt] the ball before it touched the ground." - *past-tense verb changes form*
"Catching worms is easy, but catching rats is not easy."
"His baseball team cheered when he made the catch." - *noun*

miss = *to fail to capture or hit something that is moving or falling.*
"I think he will miss the ball when he tries to hit it."
"You were right. He missed [mist] the ball."

"He keeps missing the ball when he tries to hit it!."

"That was another miss." - *noun*

swing = *moving your arm(s), or an object, in a rotating or circular motion.*

"Watch me swing the golf club."

"I swung too many times. Now my arms hurt!" - *past-tense verb changes form*

"I'll keep swinging until I hit the golf ball."

"Finally! A good swing!" - *noun*

Exercise: *Choose at least three verbs from this group, and make three sentences. Use as many subject and objects nouns as you like.*

Verbs that use our entire body.

twist = *rotating your body, or part of your body.*

"I twist my body to see what is behind me."

"She twisted [TWIS-ted] her arm to catch the falling book."

"He is twisting the screw to make it tighter."

"The bottle top needs a twist to remove it from the bottle." - *noun*

bend = *changing the angle of body parts at the joints (the parts where 2 bones meet).*

"If you do not bend your elbow, your arm will remain straight."

"She bent (*past-tense verb*) her elbow, and now her arm is bent *(adjective).*"

"Now she is bending her elbow to make her arm straight again."

"She moved her arm to create a bend." - *noun*

stretch = *extending (making longer) muscles, tendons, and joints.*

"I had to stretch my arm to reach the ball under the table."

"I stretched [stretcht] my neck, and now I feel more relaxed."

"You should keep stretching your legs when you travel for a long time."

"A tall person has a higher stretch than a short person." - *noun*

Exercise: *Choose one verb from this group, and make three sentences. Use the same verb in three different tenses: present, past and future.*

Verbs for how we move.

stand up straight [strayt] - *phrasal verb = stand as tall as possible.*
"Soldiers have to stand up straight for inspection."

lean over or **bend over** - *phrasal verbs = bend from the waist, legs straight.*
"He leaned over to pick up his pencil." - *past tense*
"She bent over to touch the water" - *past tense*

kneel down [neel] - *phrasal verb = put one or both knees on the floor.*
"We kneel down when we speak to the king and queen."
"The boy knelt [nelt] down to tie his shoes." - *past tense*
"She is kneeling down to pick flowers."

crouch down [krowch] - *phrasal verb = make your body shorter by bending the knees, the waist, the neck, or all of those parts.*
"I had to crouch down so I could reach under the tree and pick up the fallen apples."
"The children crouched [krowcht] down behind the table to hide from their friend." - *past tense*
"They are crouching down to look at the wild animals. They do not want to scare them away."

duck, or **duck down** = *make your body shorter by bending the neck, the waist, or both parts. We 'duck' so we can hide, or so something will not hit our head.*
"I duck my head when I walk under the tree branch."
"I had to duck down in the cave so I didn't hit my head on the rocks."
"We ducked when the eagle attacked us." - *past tense*

stoop, stoop down or **stooped over** [stoopt] = *standing, but the upper back and shoulders are bent forward.*
"Old people often stoop when they are standing up."
"He is stooped over and walking very slowly."

"I stooped down because I became dizzy."

Exercise: Choose three of the phrases and make three sentences. Use yourself or someone that you know as the subjects.

shuffle [SHUH-ful] = *to slide your feet on the floor when walking.*
"My grandmother shuffles her feet when she walks."
"I think the boy is sick, because he shuffled [SHUF-fuld] to bed"
"He is walking slowly and shuffling his feet."
"We knew the rat was in the box because we could hear the shuffle of its feet." - *noun*

crawl [krawl] = *to move by 'walking' with hands and knees [neez] on the floor, or move by sliding the entire body across the floor, pulling forward with hands, and pushing with knees and feet.*
"A baby will crawl before it can walk."
"The soldiers crawled [krawld] under the wire fence."
"A snake is crawling under the door."
- *'crawl' can't be a noun used this way*

limp = *one leg or foot is hurt or injured, and it causes pain when walking. When we walk, we 'limp' because it hurts on that side.*
"I cut my foot from broken glass, and I had to limp to my home."
"He limped to the doctor after his bicycle fell down."
"She is limping because her leg is hurt."
"That man walks with a limp." - *noun*

tiptoe = *walk on your toes, not your feet. We do this when we want to walk quietly, or be taller.*
"We need to tiptoe so we don't wake-up our parents."
"She tiptoed [TIP-toad] to the bathroom because the floor was wet."
"He stood on his tiptoes to reach the tallest box." - *always a plural noun*

9

sneak = *walk quietly so other people cannot see or hear us.*
"In the nighttime, I sneak into the kitchen for a snack."
"She snuck around the back of the house to meet her friend." *-past tense changes form*
"The dog is sneaking food from the table."
"My brother is a sneak! He takes my pencil when I am not looking." *- noun*

hide = *to keep from being seen. Can be a person or a thing.*
"We should hide behind the door so the teacher will not see us."
"I hid the money in my backpack." *- past tense changes form*
"She is hiding a piece of candy in her hand."
"They will look for hidden treasure." *- adjective*

Exercise: Choose three of the verbs and make three sentences. Use past tense or future tense forms of the verbs.

To say something '*out loud*' means to speak the words. This is an important way to practice pronunciation. If you have a voice recorder on your phone, record the sound of your voice as you speak. Then, listen to the recording and share it with your friends (if you are not too shy!).

Some of the exercises will ask you to '*say it out loud*'. You don't really have to say it 'loudly', but speak the words so that you can hear yourself speaking. Compare your pronunciation to the videos on YouTube. To find our YouTube videos, look for the **English Everyday** channel on YouTube.

How we react to surprises

gasp [gasp] = *a quick vocal sound when we are surprised or scared. Not using words, only a sound when we quickly breathe air in.*

"I could hear him gasp when his telephone fell out of his pocket."

"She gasped when she saw the spider in her coffee cup."

"He made a loud gasping sound when he heard the bad news." - *adjective*

"We heard his last gasp before he disappeared into the water." - *noun*

jerk = *an involuntary movement to avoid something dangerous or scary, or pulling something or someone very quickly.*

"Don't jerk the table when you sit down, or the food and drinks will spill."

"I jerked [jerkt] my leg when I saw the snake under the table."

"She was jerking her brother's arm to keep him from touching her toys."

"He had a bad dream, and woke up with a jerk." - *noun*

flinch = *a reaction to avoid being hit by something, or because something surprises us.*

Your body 'jumps' very quickly because you are surprised.

"You will flinch if a bat flies close to your face."

"He flinched [flincht] when his friend threw a rock at him." - *past tense*

"Loud sounds like guns and fireworks always make me flinch."

"Her brother scared her, and her sudden flinch caused her to fall out of the chair." - *noun*

Verbs for body functions.

burp [berp] = *gas or air from your stomach [STUM-eck] comes out your mouth.*

"I always burp after I drink Coca-Cola."

"My friend burped [burpt] more than me."

"We are burping at the same time."

"That burp was really loud!" - *noun*

belch = *a bigger, louder, longer burp.*

"My father would always belch after he ate dinner."

"He belched [belcht] as loud as he could."

"He can say words when he is belching!"

sneeze = *air comes quickly and strongly out your mouth and nose, and can be very loud and sudden.*

"My mother will sneeze when she cooks spicy food."

"My brother sneezed [sneezd] a lot when he was a baby."

"His sneezing can be so loud that, sometimes, it can scare people!"

"His loudest sneeze ever was in his English class at his school." - *noun*

cough [koff] = *air comes quickly and strongly out your mouth because of irritation in the lungs or throat.*

"I always cough when I breathe smoke from a fire."

"She coughed [koft] from the smoke too."

"He is coughing too much. I think he is sick."

"Sometimes, my cough can make me cry." - *noun*

hiccup [HICK-up] = *a sudden spasm in your belly, causing a loud, quick sucking sound.*

It can repeat many times.

"My brother can hiccup for 20 minutes when he eats too much food."

"He hiccuped [HICK-upt] for about 5 minutes yesterday."

"He's hiccupping [HICK-up-ing] and he can't stop!"

"It sounds funny when people talk during a hiccup." - *noun*

sigh [sy] = *making a sound when breathing out. A voluntary reaction when we are tired, frustrated, sad or happy. No words are used, only a sound.*

"Seeing her new grandchild made the old woman sigh with happiness."

"He sighed [side] with sadness when he dropped his telephone into the water."

"The girls were all sighing [SY-ing] when they saw the cute puppy."

"I let out a sigh of relief when the airplane landed safely." - *noun*

blink = *quickly closing and opening both eyes at the same time. An involuntary action.*

"I blink more often when I am feeling sleepy."

"I blinked [blinkt] my eyes many times during the movie."

"The baby is blinking her eyes often. I think that she is tired."

"We watch our baby girl's every blink." - *noun*

wink = *quickly closing and opening one eye as a message to someone. A voluntary action.*

"I wink at my girlfriend to embarrass her."

"She told my mother a story, and she winked at me to show that the story was not true."

"He is winking his eye at the beautiful girl."

"A wink can be an effective message." - *noun*

squint [skwint] = *closing your eyes, but not all the way closed, usually when looking at a bright light.*

"When I wake up in the morning, I squint because the light is very bright."

"He squinted to try to recognize the person walking in the fog."

"She was squinting her eyes because she just got out of bed."

"If you can't see something clearly, try giving it a squint." - *noun*

***Exercise:** Choose three verbs from this group, and make three sentences. Use one (or more) of the following adverbs in each sentence:* **quickly, always, loudly, occasionally, constantly, sometimes, loudly.**
When you are finished writing, **say it out loud** *so you can hear your own voice!*

Other verbs for body functions.

shed = *to lose hair or skin.*

"I usually shed some hair when the weather changes."

"The snake shed its skin under the house." - *past-tense verb is the same form*

"The dog is shedding its hair."

- *'shed' cannot be used as a noun in this way*

wake up / awaken [ah-WAY-ken] = *finish sleeping*

"Tell your brother to wake up. It's time to go to school."

"Your father will awaken soon."

- *cannot be used as a noun. The adjective is 'awake' [ah-WAKE].*

get up / get out of bed = *often the first action after sleep is finished.*
"It's time for all the children to get up. No more sleeping!"
"Go tell your father to get out of bed. He needs to go to work soon."
- *no noun for this one!*

Exercise: Choose one verb from this group, and make a sentence in future tense or present tense.

'**Based on**' is a term used in this book, and it is important to understand because 'based on' is used in some of the definitions. It means 'the origin of' or 'where the word, action or idea comes from'.

Examples: "This movie is based on a book about a boy and a dog."
- *The book came first, and the movie is similar to the story in the book.*

"My actions are based on my experiences."
- *The choices to do things (actions) are because of actions in the past. If an action had a good result, do it again. If there was a bad result in the past, do not do it again in the future.*

"Based on my earlier visit, I would eat at that restaurant again."
- *The speaker has been to that restaurant and enjoyed the food, and is telling the listener to eat there."*

"Many words in the English language are based on the Latin language."
- *The word 'transform' is based on two words in Latin. 'trans', which means 'across' or 'beyond', and 'forma', which means 'figure' or 'appearance'.*

Verbs for making music.

sing = *to speak the words of a song with the musical notes.*
"He can sing a Michael Jackson song."
"She sang the same song yesterday." - *past-tense verb changes form*
"We will be singing together tomorrow."
- *the noun for 'sing' is 'song', and a gerund noun is 'singing'.*

hum = *to make the notes of a song without singing or opening your mouth.*
"I don't remember the words, but I can hum the tune."
"You hummed [humd] that song before, didn't you?"
"Yes, and later today, I will be humming it again!"
"His hum is not very good, is it?" - *noun*

whistle [WHISS-el] = *to make the notes of a song by blowing air through your lips.*
"My father likes to whistle."
"He whistled [WHISS-eld] songs to me when I was a baby."
"I will be whistling to my own baby someday."
"My baby likes the sound of my whistle." - *noun*

snap your fingers = *quickly sliding one finger against your thumb to create a snapping sound.*
"Some people like to snap their fingers when they sing."
"My friend snapped [snapt] his fingers when he danced."
"I will not be snapping MY fingers when I either sing OR dance!"
"I can't make a snap with my fingers." - *'snap' used as a noun*

tap your foot = *making a sound with the bottom of your foot as it slaps the floor,* with the tempo (same time) of the song.
"I tap my foot when I hear an exciting song."
"He tapped [tapt] his foot, and he wanted to dance."
"He is tapping his foot as he is listening to the music."
"I can hear the tap of his foot." - *'tap' used as a noun*

bob your head = *moving your head front to back with the tempo, or beat, of the song.*

"If I hear a good song, I like to bob my head."

"They all bobbed [bobd] their heads when the new song played on the radio."

"We are all bobbing our heads to the beat of the song."

- we cannot use 'bob' as a noun

Exercise: *Choose two actions from this group, and make two sentences. Use at least one of the following adverbs in each sentence:* **quickly, beautifully, terribly, slowly, excitedly.**

Verbs to use for making food.

mix [miks] = *to add two or more things together.*

"To make a cake, you will need to mix several [SEV-er-al] ingredients [in-GREE-dee-ents] together."

"I mixed [mixt] eggs, flour [flower] and water to make a white sauce [soss]."

"She is mixing [MIKS-ing] the vegetables [VEJ-eh-ta-buls] for the salad [SAL-ed]."

"All the flavors create a great mix." *- 'mix' as a noun*

combine [kom-BINE] = *to add two or more things together.*

"She will combine several fruits to make a mixed-fruit pie."

"Tomatoes, garlic and herbs [erbs] are used in Italian pasta sauce."

"Indian curry is made by combining many dry spice powders."

"Thai food is a combination [kom-bin-A-shun] of vegetables, spices, curry and rice."

- 'combination' is the noun for the verb 'combine'

stir [ster] = *to combine two or more things by rotating a spoon or a stick.*

"She will stir the pot to mix the soup."

"After she stirred the pot, she put the top on it."

"In five minutes, she will be stirring the pot again."

"She gave the soup a quick stir." *- noun*

blend = *to combine two or more things by rotating a spoon or a stick, or using a blender.*

"I like to blend several different spices when I make curry."

"Today, I blended garlic, black pepper, basil and chili powder."

"Blending spices together makes a nice smell in the kitchen."

"This is a delicious blend!" - *noun*

chop = *to cut something into pieces with a knife [nyf] using a strong downward motion.*

"He will chop the vegetables after he cleans them."

"The chopped [chopt] vegetables will be mixed for a salad."

"A wooden chopping board is a good thing to chop on." - *chopping is used as an adjective*

"A strong chop will cut an onion quickly." - *noun*

slice [slyse] = *to cut something, or cut something into thin vertical pieces.*

"My mother likes to slice tomatoes very thin."

"She has already sliced ten tomatoes."

"She will continue slicing until she is finished." - *'slicing' is used as a gerund [JAIR-und] (a verb used as a noun.) See the information about 'gerunds' at the bottom of this page.*

"I want a thin slice of that tomato." - *noun*

dice [dyse] = *to cut something into small, square shaped pieces.*

"Could you dice this carrot for me?"

"I have already diced [dyst] the carrot."

"Both of us are dicing carrots!"

-'dice' cannot be used as a noun for cutting things

pour [pore] = *to cause liquid to flow by changing the angle of the container.*

"I will pour water from that bottle into this plastic cup."

"She slowly poured [pord] the oil onto the salad."

"Be careful when pouring hot liquid. If it spills, you can scald [skawld] your skin."

-no noun for 'pour'

Exercise: *Choose three verbs from this group and make three sentences. Then, speak and repeat each sentence 5 times.*

What is a 'gerund'?

gerund [JAIR-und] *is a verb word that is used as a noun in a sentence. Gerunds always end with '-ing'.*

Examples of gerund nouns used in sentences:
"I like **running**." - *'like' is the verb in this short sentence.*

Let's replace 'running' with other nouns that cannot be mistaken for verbs:
"I like food." "I like dogs." "I like sunny weather."
"What other things do you like?"
"I like **eating**, **sleeping**, and **dreaming**." *In this sentence, 'eating', 'sleeping' and 'dreaming' are the gerunds, or object nouns, of what the person 'likes'.*
If the sentence was changed a little bit... "I like **running** to my school", *the word 'running' is a verb, and 'like' becomes a helping verb.*
Three more examples of gerunds are:
"Does my **singing** bother you?"
"I like everything about her, except her **snoring**."
"**Boxing** is my favorite sport."

Verbs used for how things move.

rotate [ROH-tayt] = *to move in a circle around a center point. To spin.*
"Sometimes, leaves rotate when they fall from the trees."
"The earth rotates around the sun, and the moon rotates around the earth."
"The dancer rotated as she jumped into the air."
"Daytime and nighttime are caused by the rotation [roh-TAY-shun] of the earth." - *noun*

revolve [ree-VOLV] = *to move in a circle around a center point. To spin.*

"Wheels on a car revolve around the axles."

"The cow revolved around the grinding stone as the farmer added more corn."

"The moon is constantly revolving around the earth."

"The revolution [rev-o-LOO-shun] of the wheels creates a spinning motion." - *noun*

spin = *a revolving motion. A rotating motion.*

"My bicycle's wheels spin when I ride it."

"The wheels spun in the mud, but the car did not move." -*past-tense verb*

"My head feels like it's spinning sometimes."

"The spin of the wheels." - *noun*

Other words and phrases similar to spin, rotate and revolve - **roll around, go around the outside of, wrap around, spiral.**

twist = *spinning both ends in opposite directions.*

"A rope is made by twisting many small fibers together."

"A cable is made from twisted wires." -*adjective*

"She is twisting her hair because she is nervous about her test result."

"The twist of the rope." - *noun*

curl = *to move in a curving shape, creating a spiral [SPY-ral].*

"She wants to curl her hair. She does not like her hair to be straight [strayt]."

"The paper is curled because it was wet."

"The leaf is curling as it gets drier *[dry-er = more dry]*."

"Curls of smoke came up from the fire." - *plural noun*

swirl [swerl] and **twirl** [twerl] = *spinning or revolving to create a motion or a pattern.*

"He will swirl the sand on the table to make a circle [SER-kel] pattern."

"She twirled [twerld] in a circle until she was dizzy."

"The boy is swirling the ice cream in the bowl."

"She is wearing a red shirt with a blue swirl design." - *adjective*

wrap [rap] = *to cover a thing with another thing to hide it from view or to protect it. Or, to spin a thing around another thing.*
"She will wrap the food with paper to protect it from insects."
"I wrapped [rapd] the gift before I went to the birthday party."
"My father is wrapping [rapping] a bandage around his arm."
"Plastic wrap is good for helping to keep food fresh." - *noun*

wind [wine + a quick 'd' sound. use a long 'i' sound…'eye'] = *wrap something around another thing with a rotating, circular motion.*
"If you have an old-style watch or clock, you need to wind it."
"I wound [wownd] the rope around the tree." - *the past-tense verb changes form*
"He is winding a string around a piece of wood."
"Each wind of the wire should be very tight." - *noun*

loop = *to wind [long 'i' sound, like 'eye'] into a circle or oval shape.*
"Loop the rope around your arm."
"The snake looped [loopt] itself into a circle shape."
"My kite string is looping around that tree branch."
"The loops of the rope create a circle shape." - *noun*

Similar words to **'twist'**, 'curl', 'swirl' and 'twirl' – **coil, spiral, helix, coil, serpentine** ("S" curves).

Exercise: *Choose two verbs from this group, and make two sentences. Find something to create a 'looping' action. Use a rope, a string or a rubber band and 'loop' it around your finger. You can 'twist' or 'curl' a piece of paper. Speak the sentence as you make the action.*

wiggle [WIGG-el] = *move from side to side or up and down. Can be fast or slow. Can be voluntary or involuntary.*
"When my tooth is loose, I can wiggle it with my fingers."
"The boy wiggled in the chair as his mother tried to cut his hair."
"She is wiggling the strawberry jam in the bowl."

"Look at the wiggle of my tooth!" - *noun*

wriggle [RIGG-el] = *a twisting motion from side to side. Can be fast or slow. Always a voluntary movement.*
"If I pick up the fish, it will wriggle until I drop it."
"The dancer wriggled [RIGG-eld] her body without moving her feet."
"The baby goat was wriggling its body when I picked it up."
"I like the wriggle of the dancer's belly." - *noun*

jiggle [JIGG-el] = *a short, fast back and forth or up and down movement. Can be voluntary or involuntary.*
"Gelatin will jiggle if you shake the bowl."
"He jiggled [JIGG-eld] the key in the lock to open the door."
"The fat man's belly is jiggling when he walks."
"The jiggle of his big belly made us laugh" - *noun*

squirm [skwerm] = *wriggle to escape, or because of discomfort. Always a voluntary movement.*
"If you hold a snake, it will squirm to escape."
"She squirmed [skwermd] with fear when she saw the big spider."
"The smaller boy is squirming to escape from the bigger boy."
"The snake's squirm is very fast." - *noun*

writhe [rythe] = *a random, involuntary motion (squirming) because of discomfort or pain. Always an involuntary movement.*
"Pain caused by his broken leg bone made him writhe on the floor."
"She writhed [rythd] in pain from her injury."
"The doctor could not examine the boy's injury because the boy was writhing in pain."
- *there is no noun for 'writhe'.*

Exercise: *Choose three verbs from this group, and make three sentences. Use your body to make the movements as you say what you are doing.*

21

tremble [TREM-bul] = *all or part of the body shaking because of discomfort, fear, or cold. Always an involuntary movement.*

"I tremble at the thought of being in a graveyard at night."

"Her entire body trembled when the cold wind started to blow."

"The children were trembling with fear after they heard a screaming sound."

"Seeing that woman's trembles make me feel cold too." - *noun*

quiver [KWIV-er] = *a slight, rapid motion of a small area of the body, or a thing. Always an involuntary movement.*

"His arms started to quiver as he lifted the heavy bucket above his head."

"The leaves on the trees quivered in the breeze."

"When an insect is in its web, a spider can feel the quiver of the web." - *noun*

shiver [SHIV-er] = *all or part of the body shaking involuntarily because of cold or sickness.*

"Even though the air was hot, she started to shiver from the high fever."

"He shivered when I threw ice-cold water on his shirt."

"We were shivering because we did not wear warm clothes."

"Influenza can give you the shivers." - *noun*

twitch = *part of the body shaking because of muscle spasm or nervousness. Always an involuntary movement.*

"Her foot was twitching, and she could not stop it."

"The prisoner twitched in his chair as the policeman demanded answers."

"I have a little twitch in my eyelid." - *noun*

spasm [SPAZZ-um] = *small movements or contractions in muscle [MUSS-el] tissue.*

Always an involuntary movement.

"Sometimes, my muscles spasm in my lower back."

"His stomach spasmed [SPAZZ-umd] until he vomited."

"The muscles in her arm were spasming for two hours."

"A muscle spasm in your leg can make it impossible to walk." - *noun*

fidget [FID-jet] = *small body movements caused by impatience or nervousness.*
"The children will begin to fidget if we make them wait too long."
"He fidgeted [FID-jeh-ted] when the police took him to the crime scene."
"The suspect would not stop fidgeting as the policeman questioned him."
"His fidgets were evidence of guilt." - *noun*

shake (involuntary) = *all or part of the body moving in quick, short motions because of muscle spasm, nervousness, or cold.*
"She will shake with fear when she sees a spider."
"His body shook [sounds like 'book'] when I scared him." - *past-tense verb changes form*
"His arms are shaking from digging the dirt all day."
"I noticed the shake of fear when he saw his ex-girlfriend." - *noun*

shake (voluntary) = *all or part of the body moving in quick, short motions.*
"When people meet, they often shake hands."
"He shook [sounds like 'book'] the bottle before he opened it." - *past-tense verb*
"She is shaking the box to guess what is inside."
"His quick shake caused the liquid to spray out of the bottle." - *noun*

Exercise: *Choose four verbs from this group, and make two sentences. Use two of the verbs in each sentence.*

bounce [bown-sss] = *something moves quickly, hits a surface, and goes back in the opposite direction.*
"The ball will bounce if you drop it on the floor."
"He bounced the balloon on his brother's head."
"Can you try bouncing a coin into a cup?"
"Dropping an egg will not result in a bounce." - *noun*

Exercise: *Find something that can bounce, and another thing that cannot bounce. Make two sentences about those two things.*

Verbs used for moving something.

These are literal meanings for the words. Many of these words are also used in metaphorical phrases. We will discuss metaphors and metaphorical phrases in another English Everyday book.

pull = *use your hand(s) to bring something closer, or to open or close something.*
"You can pull the string to ring the bell."
"He pulled [puld] my arm and I almost fell down."
"The tractor is pulling the car out of the mud."
"A strong pull will make a buffalo move." - *noun*

push = *use your hand(s) to move something further away, or to open or close something.*
"Push the door to open it."
"She pushed [poosht] her brother away from her toys."
"He is pushing me towards the swimming pool."
"My car needs a push to start moving." - *noun*

jerk = *a strong, fast, short pull.*
"Please don't jerk my hair. It hurts!"
"He jerked [jerkt] my arm to save me from the speeding car."
"He is jerking his little brother's finger."
"The final jerk caused his tooth to fall out." - *noun*

tug = *a fast, short pull. usually a tug is for a thing, not a person.*
"If we tug the rope, the horse will follow us."
"He got my attention when he tugged [tugd] on my jacket."
"The small boat is tugging the bigger boat."
"If you give the door a strong tug, it will close all the way." - *noun*

Exercise: *Choose either 'jerk' or 'tug', and make two past-tense sentences.*

"Helping" verbs.

Helping verbs, also called **auxiliary verbs** or **modal verbs**, are words that work together with active verbs to help communicate the message or meaning. Here are some examples. You will see that the sentence with the helping verb is more specific than the sentence with no helping verb.

"I am going to the market." - *Not specific about a time. Are you going now, later today, or next week?*

"I will go to the market." - *Not specific about a time. We know that you have not gone yet, but we do not know when you plan to go. The helping verb is 'will'.*

"I will go to the market at 4 o'clock today." - *We know exactly when you will go!*

Using the simple sentence **"go to the beach today"**, *we can see how the message changes when we use different helping verbs:*

"We **can** go to the beach today."
"We **will** go to the beach today."
"We **might** go to the beach today."
"We **must** go to the beach today."
"We **need to** go to the beach today."
"We **have to** go to the beach today."
"We **could** go to the beach today."
"We **would** go to the beach today, but it is raining!"

All of these examples are about the same subject, going to the beach, but each sentence has a different message. **Must, need to,** and **have to** are similar meanings, but the others have very different meanings.

Other helping verbs are: **do, be, may, have, should, shall, ought to** [ott to]**, and dare to.**

This sentence is an answer to the question "Do you go to the beach sometimes?"
"Yes, we **do** go to the beach sometimes."
These are past-tense examples:
"We **went** to the beach already."
"We **have gone** to the beach already."
"We **have been** to the beach already."

These are examples of helping verbs for future actions:
"We **may** go to the beach tomorrow." "We **might** go to the beach tomorrow."
- these two are the same meaning.

"We **ought to** go to the beach tomorrow." "We **should** go to the beach tomorrow."
- these two are the same meaning

"We **will be** going to the beach tomorrow." "We **shall be** going to the beach tomorrow."
- these two are the same meaning

"We **will dare to** go to the beach tomorrow."
- 'dare' means 'taking a risk or a challenge'. Maybe their car is old, or the weather might be bad.

- 'used to' means something happened in the past and now it does not happen, or you had something in the past and now you do not have it.
"We **used to** go to the beach, but now we don't go there."

Verbs used for changing the form or shape of things.

scrape = *use a tool to damage the surface of something, or remove something from a surface.*

"He used a knife to scrape his name on the table."

"The tree scraped [skraypt] the skin off of my arms when I fell."

"I am scraping the old paint off of the chair."

"There is a scrape on my car from the accident." - *noun*

scratch = *use a tool, an object, or fingernails, to damage something, or relieve itching.*

"Don't scratch a mosquito bite. You can damage your skin."

"The paint on the table was scratched [skratcht] by the broken glass."

"The boy is scratching his head because he can't think of the answer."

"My new refrigerator has a scratch on the front side." - *noun*

smash = *use a strong force or a tool to make something break apart, or change the shape.*

"The boy likes to smash his food when he eats it."

"The car was smashed [smasht] by a very big rock."

"Because of the storm, there are trees falling down and smashing on our house."

"He slipped and fell when he stepped on the smashed banana." - *adjective*

crush = *use a strong force or a tool to make something break apart, make it smaller, or change the shape.*

"A big truck can crush a small car."

"We watched as the elephant crushed [krusht] our tent with its foot."

"She is crushing the medicine into powder with a spoon."

"The toy car was destroyed with the crush of my foot." - *noun*

Exercise: Choose two verbs from this group, and make two future-tense sentences. Also, use one of these adverbs in each sentence: **loudly, strongly, quietly, quickly, effortlessly.**

squeeze [skweez] = *use hand(s) or a tool to compress or constrict something (see below).*

"Don't squeeze the baby rabbit. You can hurt it!"

"I squeezed [skweezd] the lemon to make the juice come out."

"His hands were squeezing my neck."

"Her hand began to hurt because of her father's strong squeeze." - *noun*

compress [kom-PRESS] = *to make something smaller by using pressure or force, or by taking away extra information.*

"I will compress the box when I sit on it."

"Gasses can be compressed [kom-PREST] and put in cans. Spray paint is an example"

"Her story is too long, so she is compressing it by taking some words away."

"I will send a compressed file as an e-mail attachment." - *adjective*

constrict [kon-STRIKT] = *squeezing with pressure to make something smaller, stop from moving, or prevent from doing something.*

"Some kinds of snakes constrict other animals to kill them."

"His shirt was too small, and it constricted [kon-STRIK-ted] his fat belly"

"The walls of the cave became narrower, constricting the man's ability to move forward."

"Eating too much fat and oil will cause constricted blood vessels." - *adjective*

flatten = [FLAT-ten] = *to smash or compress something until it is flat.*

"Could you flatten this can with your foot?"

"His hat was flattened by a bus."

"The crushing machine is flattening the old car."

"The flattened old car will be recycled." - *adjective*

Exercise: *Choose one verb from this group, and make three sentences with the same verb using: past continuous, present continuous and future continuous verb tenses.*

raze [rays] = *burn a structure until it is destroyed.*

"The city plans to raze the old part of the town and build a new school."

"Many homes were razed by the big fire."

"Be careful with the fire. We don't want to be razing our home!"

"The razed buildings were still smoking after two weeks." - *adjective*

bulldoze [BULL-doze] = *to push down a structure, or trees, using a tractor or a bulldozer.*

"They plan to bulldoze the home and sell the property."

"The home was bulldozed yesterday."

"The workers are bulldozing the home now."

"A bulldozer was used to destroy the homes." - *noun*

topple [TOP-ul] = *fall down.*

"A tall building will topple if it is not designed correctly."

"I toppled the stack of chairs when I fell down."

"The old man keeps toppling when he tries to walk."

"We had to pick up all the toppled books." - *adjective*

Exercise: *Take a break and go outside for ten minutes!*

Verbs used for cleaning things.

sweep = *use your hand, a broom or a brush to move dirt, dust, or something else from a surface.*

"The children said that they would sweep the floor after the party."

"She swept the dust off of the clothes with her hand." - *the past-tense verb changes form*

"You are responsible for sweeping the spider webs on the ceiling."

"This broom makes a much wider sweep that that broom." - *noun*

brush off = *use your hand, a broom, or a brush, to move dirt or dust from a surface.*

"Can you brush off the table before we eat?"

"She brushed off [brusht off] the cookie crumbs from her skirt."

"My father is brushing the dirt off of his car."

- *because 'brush off' is a phrasal verb, there is no noun.*

wash = *to clean, usually with water and soap.*

"Wash your hands before dinner!"

"She washed [washt] her cat in the sink."
"Washing a car is *not* my favorite thing to do."
"This dirty shirt needs a wash." - *noun*

scrub = *quick, strong side-to-side motion using a cloth or a brush, usually for cleaning.*
"I need to scrub the blanket to take the coffee stain away."
"She scrubbed [shrubd] the floor for fifteen minutes."
"I am scrubbing the bottom of the pot."
"The dirt will not come out without a strong scrubbing." - *gerund*

rub = *make a circular or back-and-forth motion using the palm of the hand.*
"I will rub salt onto the meat before I cook it."
"She rubbed [rubbd] the spot on her arm where her brother hit her."
"The boy smiled and rubbed his hands together when he saw the food on the table."
"My back hurts. I need a good rub." - *noun*

polish [POLL-ish] = *rub a smooth surface to make it shiny.*
"Use a piece of cloth to polish to polish the plates."
"He polished [POLL-isht] his motorcycle until it looked like new."
"Will you be finished polishing soon?"
"The surface of the polished marble looked like glass." - *adjective*

Exercise: *Make a sentence using one of the verbs, but use the word as a gerund. A gerund is a verb that ends in -ing, and works as a noun in the sentence, so you will also need to choose another verb! Use the gerund as the last word in the sentence.*

wring [ring] = *twist a wet cloth to squeeze the water out.*
"You can wring the wet towel to make it drier."
"He came inside from the rain and wrung [rung] his shirt."
- the past-tense verb changes form
"The girl is wringing her school uniform to make it dry quickly."
- no noun for 'wring'

30

Exercise: make a sentence with 'wring' as a future-tense verb, and a sentence using 'massage' as a past-tense verb.

Verbs used when something cannot be seen, heard or understood clearly.

block = *something moves between you and what you are looking at.*
"Please don't block my view of the movie."
"The woman's umbrella blocked [blokt] the sunshine."
"He could not score a goal because the other player was blocking his shot."
"Trees are a natural block for wind, sun and rain." - *noun*

obscure [ob-SKYOOR] = *try to prevent from being seen or understood. Not commonly used as a verb.*
"They are trying to obscure the details of their crime."
"We could not see him clearly because he was obscured [ob-SKYOORD] by fog."
"His lies are obscuring what really happened."
"There are many obscure actors in Hollywood." - *adjective - it means 'not well known' or 'not popular'*

hide = *something is trying to not be seen, or someone does not want you to see it.*
"Quickly, hide the money in your bag!"
"The children hid in the bedroom." - *the past-tense verb changes form*
"We were hiding in the forest."
"They needed to find a good hiding place." - *adjective*

Exercise: make a sentence with 'block' or 'obscure', and use the past-tense form of the verb.

keep out of sight = *hide.*
"We have to keep out of sight so our parents can't find us."
"Some rooms in the Taj Mahal are kept out of sight, and never seen by most visitors."
"Keep the children out of sight when the guests arrive."

- because 'keep out of sight' is a prepositional phrase, there is no noun

conceal [kon-SEEL] = *hide.*
"He wants to conceal the diamond ring so his girlfriend does not see it."
"The police concealed [kon-SEELD] the name of the murderer so the man's family would not be bothered."
"The pyramids in Egypt are concealing the burial [BARE-ee-al] chambers of kings and queens."
"She found her husband's concealed money." - *adjective. it means 'hidden'*

cloud = *something cannot be seen, or clearly understood, because of a distraction.*
"Don't let your opinion about cloud your choices."
"The smoke from the fire clouded [KLOUD-ed] the view of the valley."
"His anger is clouding his judgement. If he starts a fight, the police will arrest him."
"The magician [mah-JISH-an] disappeared in a cloud of smoke." - *noun*

cover [KUV-er] = *something is on top of, in front of, or protecting something.*
"Please cover the salad bowl with a plate."
"A big hat covered [KUV-erd] his head, protecting him from the weather."
"A cloth is covering the old car."
"The hole in the roof needs a cover so the water can't come inside." - *noun*

screen = *something between you and what you are looking at, but maybe you CAN see through it.*
"Could you screen the cookies so the children will not see them?"
"She stood between me and my friend, and screened [skreend] his view."
"The trees were screening my shot. I could not shoot the deer."
"Please, stand in front of me as a screen." - *noun*

mask = *something between you and what you are looking at that changes the appearance.*
"I will mask the car with mud so it cannot be seen."
"They masked [maskt] their faces with paint to keep from being recognized."

"We are masking the view of the factory by planting trees."

"Halloween is a popular holiday. Children wear a scary or funny mask over their faces." - *noun*

shroud [shrowd] = *hidden from understanding, or difficult to see the details.*

"Why does he always shroud his stories with lies?"

"The top of mountain is shrouded [SHROW-ded] by the clouds."

"Shrouding the truth is a common tactic in politics."

"The dead man was wrapped in a white shroud." - *noun*

veil [vail] = *a thin covering that prevents a clear view, or a story that hides the truth.*

"The woman wore a veil, making it difficult to see her face."

"The details of political corruption are veiled [vaild] with deception."

"Tomorrow will be the unveiling of the new monument." - unveiling means to reveal, or show, something

"We can't see the statue until the veil is taken off." - *noun*

Exercise: *Choose three of these 'hiding' verbs, and make three sentences. Do not use the same subject each time!*

wrap [rap] = *cover something with paper, plastic or fabric.*

"She will wrap the food with plastic so it does not get dry."

"I wrapped [rapt] the birthday gift with paper so she could not see what was inside."

"The mother is wrapping a towel around the baby."

"Is this paper okay to use for gift wrap?" - *noun*

sequester [seh-KWEST-er] = *to hide a person or a thing so it cannot be contacted. Not commonly used.*

"The members of the trial jury were sequestered [seh-KWEST-erd] in a hotel to prevent them from hearing evidence that might change their opinions. They had no access to information, news, gossip or hearsay." -past-tense

eclipse [ee-KLIPS] = *hidden or overtaken by something that is relatively bigger, more popular or more important.*
"News about a war will eclipse news about the weather."
"America's economy may be eclipsed [ee-KLIPST] by China's economy in the future."
"The new James Bond movie is eclipsing the new Spiderman movie in ticket sales."
"The next total eclipse of the sun will be in 2024." - *noun*

envelop [en-VEL-op] = *something is completely covered or surrounded.*
"A caterpillar will envelop itself with a cocoon, then transform into a butterfly."
"The Earth is enveloped [en-VEL-opt] inside of an atmosphere that can support life."
"The spider is enveloping the insect with silk before killing it."
- the noun is 'envelope' [EN-vel-ope], which is a paper container used for mailing a letter

camouflage [KAM-o-flaj] = *difficult to see because it is the same color or pattern as the background or the surroundings.*
"Many animals are the same color as their environment, and can camouflage themselves by not moving."
"Although a tiger is black, orange and white, it is camouflaged [KAM-o-flajd] in the jungle."
"The soldiers are camouflaging their faces with green paint."
"Hunters wear camouflage clothes to avoid being seen by animals." - *adjective*

Exercise: *Practice saying "**eclipse, envelop, camouflage**" using the correct emphasis. Say the three words together, ten times.*

bury [BARE-ee] = *to hide by making a hole in the ground and covering with dirt.*
"We should bury the dead dog to hide the bad smell."
"The Japanese army buried [BARE-eed] a lot of stolen gold in Burma."
"The battle is finished, and now they are burying the dead soldiers."
"The boys have a map to find the buried treasure [TREH-zhure]." - *adjective*

34

Other words and phrases that have a similar meaning to 'bury' are:
entomb [en-TOOM], **put under the ground, lay to rest, cover with earth, six feet under.**

Exercise: Talk about some things that are buried in the area that you live.

"Onomatopoeia" words.

*There is a category of words called **onomatopoeia** [on-o-maht-o-PEE-ya).*
They are words that 'sound' like an action.

ring and **ding** are sounds from a bell.

beep is the sound of a car's horn.

toot is the sound of a trumpet.

pow, **bang**, **boom** and **kapow** are sounds of a gun, or something exploding.

zap is the sound of an electric shock.

sizzle is something cooking.

brrrr is not a real word, but people say it when they are feeling cold.

snap is the sound of something cracking.

whisper is when we speak quietly, or the quiet sound of a gentle breeze.

gush is water moving quickly.

whoosh is the wind, or air blowing quickly.

buzz is the sound of a bee.

splash is the sound of something falling into water.

thump is something falling down, when it hits the floor.

zip is the sound from a zipper, or something moving fast.

zoom is the sound of something moving quickly.

hiss is the sound of a snake, or compressed air escaping from a tire.

The sounds that animals make are also **onomatopoeia** sounds.

A cow says **moo**, a cat sound is **meeow**, birds sound like **tweet tweet**, pigs say **oink**, and a sheep sounds like **baah**.

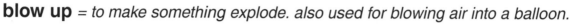

Verbs to use for things that make a loud sound.

explode [ex-PLODE] = *a quick, loud reaction caused by internal pressure.*
"A bottle of soda will explode if the pressure inside the bottle is too high."
"Many bombs are exploded to test the results."
"Terrorists have started exploding bombs in big cities."
"We heard a very loud explosion." - *noun*

blow up = *to make something explode. also used for blowing air into a balloon.*
"Don't call the police, or I will blow up the building with a bomb!"
"The bomb blew up." "The building was blown up." - *2 examples of past-tense usage*
"The boy is blowing up a balloon." - *because 'blow up' is a phrasal verb, there is no noun*

detonate [DET-uh-nate] = *the action of making a bomb explode.*
"If you don't give us what we want, we will detonate the bomb."
"When the dynamite was detonated [DET-uh-nated], we heard a huge explosion."
"Some soldiers are experts at detonating bombs safely."
"The detonation made a very loud 'bang' sound." - *noun*

erupt [ee-RUPT] = *explode with fire like a volcano, or when a fight or a war starts quickly.*
"The volcano will erupt soon."
"Suddenly, the argument erupted [ee-RUP-ted] into a fight."
"Another war is erupting in the Middle East region."
"Hot magma flowed down the mountain from the volcano's eruption." - *noun*

discharge [diss-CHARJ] = *when a gun shoots bullets, or when something is released from where it has been staying.*
"Do not discharge your gun until you are instructed to shoot."

"We heard a very loud *BOOM* when the cannon discharged [diss-CHARJD]."

"Be careful, he is discharging his pistol."

"We were startled by the sudden discharge of the gun." - *noun*

Other words for loud sounds are: **bang, pop, crash, pound, roar, boom, blast, beep, toot.**

snap = *the sound of something breaking. a cracking sound like glass or wood.*

"A small tree will snap if you try to climb [klime] it."

"His bone snapped [snapt] when he fell down."

"Tree branches are snapping and breaking because of the strong wind." - *phrasal verb*

"I heard a loud snap when my phone fell on the floor." - *noun*

Verbs used for vehicle accidents.

crash = *a vehicle accident, or the sound of something breaking.*

"The airplane will crash if the wing falls off."

"Nobody was hurt when the bus crashed [krasht] into the wall."

"I heard a crashing sound in the kitchen when the plates fell down." - *adjective*

"Did you see the car crash?" - *noun*

collide [ko-LIDE] = *something that is moving hits another object.*

"The slippery road caused the two trucks to collide."

"The car's braked did not work, and it collided [ko-LIDE-ed] into a tree."

"The researchers will be colliding atoms in the particle accelerator."

"A car was hit by a train, and it was destroyed by the collision [ko-LIZH-un]." - *noun*

wreck [rek] = *a vehicle or a machine is broken because of an accident.*

"When you drive my truck, try not to wreck it."

"She wrecked [rekd] her car yesterday."

"I think that my friend enjoys wrecking his cars."

"My motorcycle was destroyed in a wreck last month." - *noun*

Phrasal verbs that mean 'crash', 'collide or 'wreck':

run into = *something that is moving hits another object.*

smash into = *something that is moving hits another object.*

smack into = *something that is moving hits another object.*

slam into = *something that is moving quickly hits another object.*

plow into = *something that is moving quickly hits another object.*

bump into = *something that is moving slowly hits another object.*

Exercise: write two sentences with two 'accident' verbs, then read and speak the sentences. Say each sentence three times. Then, make one sentence using one of the phrasal verbs.

Verbs used for hitting.

strike = *one thing hits another thing.*

"The airplane could strike that tall tree if it flies too low."

"She struck her head on the top of the door frame." - *past tense changes form*

"One man is striking the other man with his fist."

"Our house was damaged by the lightning strike." - *noun*

impact [IM-pakt] = *one thing hits another thing, or an event affects the results.*

"An asteroid from space can impact the Earth."

"New evidence has impacted [IM-pak-ted] the opinion of the judge."

"Flooding [FLUH-ding] from the river is impacting the entire village."

"The impact of a nuclear explosion's radiation can last for many years." - *noun*

punch = *hitting with a closed hand (a fist).*

"If you punch a wall, you can hurt your hand."

"The boy punched [puncht] his older brother, then ran away."

"My nose was broken as he was punching me."

"The boxer knocked [nokt] the other fighter out with one punch." - *noun*

slap = *hitting with the palm (inside part) of an open hand.*

"When you play volleyball, you have to slap the ball when you serve."
"She slapped [slapt] her boyfriend's face because he said something rude [rood]."
"The joke was so funny that he was slapping his leg and laughing."
"A hard slap can really hurt!" - *noun*

smack = *a slap, or the sound that a slap makes.*
"The teacher will smack your hand if you don't pay attention."
"His paddle smacked [smakt] the water as he tried to hit the fish."
"We heard a smacking sound when she slapped his face." - *adjective*
"If you tickle her, she will give you a smack!" - *noun*

Exercise: choose three of the 'hitting' verbs, and make three sentences. Use your hand to make the action of the verb, but please do not hurt anyone or break anything!

Verbs to use to describe why things don't work anymore.

break = *an action that causes something to separate into pieces, or to stop working.*
"The light bulb will break if you drop it on the floor."
"He dropped the light bulb and broke it!" - *the form changes as a past-tense verb*
"Breaking light bulbs is not a good idea."
"A broken light bulb cannot be used anymore." - *adjective*

injure [IN-jur] = *to damage a thing, part of your body, your reputation, or your emotions (feelings).*
"A car accident can injure the car and the people in the car."
"He injured [IN-jurd] his arm when he slipped and fell."
"His strange behavior is injuring his reputation in the town."
"There were various injuries [IN-jur-eez] caused by the bus crash." - *noun*

damage [DAMM-aj] = *broken or injured, but can be repaired or fixed.*
"Too much sun can damage your skin."
"My telephone was damaged when I dropped it."

"Pollution is damaging the rivers and oceans."
"An accident can cause damage to your car." - *noun*

destroy [dee-STROY] = *broken and cannot be repaired or fixed.*
"A fire can destroy your home."
"In the Japanese movie, Godzilla destroyed [dee-STROYD] Tokyo."
"The dog is destroying my shoe!"
"The typhoon caused a lot of destruction [dee-STRUK-shun] in Myanmar." - *noun*

ruin [ROO-in] = *to destroy.*
"A water leak can ruin your house."
"My motorcycle was ruined [ROO-ind] by the angry elephant."
"The tornado is ruining many homes and businesses."
"The entire village is in ruins because of the fire." - *prepositional phrase*

Other words and phrases for these words: **wiped out, facing ruin, falling to pieces, in pieces, in tatters, dilapidated, on the rocks.**

Exercise: Use the verbs 'injure' and 'damage'. Write two sentences using each verb.

wreck [reck] = *to damage or destroy.*
"Please don't wreck your bicycle."
"The accident wrecked [rekd] both the truck and the house."
"Termites are wrecking my furniture."
"He saw the car wreck from his office." - *noun*

fall apart = *the pieces of something are not together anymore.*
"My shirt is beginning to fall apart."
"The pieces of the toy fell apart when he sat on it."
"The chair is falling apart."

deteriorate [dee-TEER-ee-oh-rate] = *pieces and parts are not strong, and begin to fall apart.*

"As we get older, our bodies deteriorate."

"His boat deteriorated [dee-TEER-ee-oh-rate-ed] after many years in the water."

"The books are slowly deteriorating, and the pages are falling out."

"Our wood fence is falling down because of deterioration [dee-teer-ee-oh-RAISH-on]." - *noun changes in form and emphasis*

Exercise: Make one sentence using 'deteriorate', and say it out loud three times.

break down = *pieces and parts are not strong, and begin to fall apart.*

"This machine will break down sometimes, and we can't use it until it is repaired."

"His truck broke down on the highway." - *past tense*

"My car is broken down and I cannot drive it to my work." - *adjective*

"The train tracks are breaking down from the earthquake."

shut down = *has been stopped, or closed, by someone.*

"The factory will be shut down next month."

"His business has been shut down for two years."

- *present-tense, past-tense and future tense of 'shut down' are all the same form*

dismantle [diss-MAN-tul] = *take something apart, separate the pieces.*

"We will dismantle the car so we can see all the parts."

"The boy dismantled [diss-MAN-tuld] his toy airplane."

"Engineers are dismantling the bridge so they can replace the old structure."

"We examined the dismantled air compressor." - *adjective*

More common ways to say 'dismantle' are: **take apart, pull apart, break down, strip down, separate the pieces, disassemble, pull down, knock down, deconstruct.**

Exercise: make a sentence with one of the common phrases that mean 'dismantle'.

Verbs to use when something is destroyed or taken away.

devastate [DEV-ah-state] = *cause severe damage. many things broken or destroyed.*
"A bomb will devastate anything when it explodes."
"Japan was devastated by an earthquake followed by a tsunami."
"The war in Afghanistan is devastating the traditional culture."
"In some countries in Africa, devastation from local wars can be seen." - *noun*

demolish [dee-MOLL-ish] = *cause severe damage or destruction.*
"We plan to demolish this building tomorrow."
"The men demolished [dee-MOLL-isht] the building.
"When they were demolishing the building, they found a hidden treasure."
"They discovered the treasure during the demolition [de-mo-LISH-un]. - *noun changes in form and emphasis*

obliterate [oh-BLIT-er-ate] = *to completely destroy, take away, or make invisible.*
"Sometimes, time or political leaders will obliterate the history of an entire culture."
"The Etruscan civilization in Italy was obliterated [oh-BLIT-er-ay-ted] by the Romans."
"After 40 years, the police are obliterating his criminal record."
"We found evidence of the obliterated town." - *adjective*

eradicate [ee-RAD-ih-kate] = *to take away all, or kill, all of a group of things.*
"The soldiers were ordered to eradicate the local people."
"All the animals in the forest were eradicated [ee-RAD-ih-kay-ted] by the fire."
"Doctors are eradicating malaria from the region."
"There were no signs of life after the nuclear eradication." - *noun*

erase [ee-RACE] = *to remove from view or memory.*
"Please erase the words on the blackboard."
"He erased [ee-RACEt] the drawing of a horse that he made."
"Her newly found happiness was erasing the sad feelings about her tragic past."
"Use an eraser to take the words off of the paper." - *noun*

delete [dee-LEET or deh-LEET] = *to remove from view or memory.*

42

"He will try to delete the memories of the tragedy."

"The teacher deleted [dee-LEET-ed] the boy's name from the list."

"My school is deleting geography from the currriculum."

"The editor made several deletions [dee-LEE-shuns] to the author's story." - *plural noun*

wipe out = *to take away all, or kill all.*

"Scientists believe that dinosaurs were wiped out when a huge [hyooj] meteor hit the Earth."

wipe off the face of the Earth = *all gone and will never be seen again.*

"Because of hunting and dogs, dodo birds were wiped off the face of the Earth."

remove all traces of = *all gone and will never be seen again.*

"The landslide removed all traces of the village, except for broken pieces of peoples' homes."

nuke [newk] = *there are two uses for this word.*

1. to make something hot in a microwave oven, and 2. destroy with a nuclear bomb.

"If you want to make food hot quickly, nuke it!"

"I nuked [newkt] my coffee because it was cold."

"If there is a war, I hope we don't get nuked!"

"The 'no nukes' movement supports a ban on nuclear weapons and nuclear energy."
- adjective

Words and phrases similar to these words: **liquidate** [LIK-wid-ate], **decimate** [DESS-ih-mate], **annihilate** [an-NYE-ill-ate], **blot out**, **wipe out**, **get rid of**.

Verbs used when we change the shape or size.

cut = *divided into two or more pieces using a knife, a saw, or scissors.*

"I will cut the onions, and you can cut the meat."

"Yesterday, he cut wood for the fire." - *same form for past-tense*

"The girl is cutting paper to make butterfly shapes."

"The dog has a cut on its leg." - *noun*

chop = *cut or divide using a big knife, with a strong downward motion.*

"Use a knife to chop the chicken meat."

"She is using chopped [chopt] chicken meat in the soup." - *adjective*

"He is chopping a big tree with an axe. The tree will fall down soon"

"The tree fell down after the final chop." - *noun*

sever [SEH-ver] = *remove a body part from a living thing by cutting it off.*

"The doctor had to sever the man's infected leg."

"His finger was severed [SEH-verd] when he put his hand too close to the electric saw."

"I can't watch when my father severs the fish's head."

"A bird cannot fly with a severed wing." - *adjective*

saw = *cut with a saw.*

"My brother will saw down the tree tomorrow."

"He sawed [sawd] through the wood easily."

"She is sawing through the bones of the cow to make smaller pieces of meat."

"Give me that saw so I can cut this wood." - *noun*

Exercise: *Make two sentences with two of these verbs, and use the future tense.*

When things break, we use these words.

There are many meanings for the word 'break', but we will limit the definitions in this lesson.

smash = *broken into pieces, or made flat, using a tool or something heavy.*

"I can smash the rock with a hammer."

"He threw a brick and smashed [smasht] the window."

"My father is smashing metal cans with his foot."

"We heard a loud smashing sound." - *adjective*

bash = *hit something with a heavy thing to change its shape, or break it.*
"You have to bash it harder if you want to break it."
"The car bashed [basht] into the side of the bridge."
"The boys are bashing a frog with a piece of wood."
"My car was bashed-in by a motorcycle." - *prepositional phrase or adjective*

crash = *a vehicle accident, or a smashing sound.*
"We could crash if you continue to drive too fast."
"The airplane crashed [krashd] in the forest."
"Crashing a motorcycle can be very dangerous."
"A car crash can be dangerous and expensive." - *noun*

crush = *made flatter or smaller using a tool or something heavy.*
"A falling tree can crush a house."
"I crushed [krusht] the metal cans so I could fit more into a bag."
"The machine [mah-SHEEN] is crushing rocks to make a new road."
"There were many people on the train, and everyone could feel the crush." - *the noun is more similar to the verb 'compress'*

shatter [SHAT-ter] = *a rigid material has been broken into many small pieces.*
"Glass will shatter when it breaks."
"His bone was shattered [SHAT-terd] from the accident."
"My brother is outside shattering bottles with a rock."
"The x-ray showed the shattered bone." - *adjective*

splinter [SPLIN-ter] = *slender, narrow, sharp pieces (example: wood, bone or glass) created from being broken. There are not so many things that will 'splinter' when they are broken.*
"A piece of wood will splinter when it is crushed."
"His bone was splintered [SPLIN-terd] when he fell down the mountain."
"The force of the bulldozer is splintering the tree."
"I have a splinter of broken glass in my finger." - *noun*

crack = *a surface that has been broken, but not separated.*
"The ice will crack if they walk on the frozen lake."
"Heavy trucks cracked [krakt] the surface of the road."
"The plaster is cracking as it dries."
"A can see a crack in the concrete wall." - *noun*

bust = *informal word for "break".*
"Please don't bust my favorite coffee cup."
"My brother busted [BUS-ted] my toy truck."
"I can't use this busted telephone!" - *adjective*

Other words and phrases for 'break' or 'broken' are: **malfunction, kaput, stopped working, break down, broken down, broken up, snapped off, conked out, on the blink.**

Exercise: *Choose three of these verbs and make three sentences.*

"Sense" verbs.

There are many ways to experience things. There are things that we can hear, and other things that we can see, taste, smell, or touch. Many experiences use more than one of our senses at the same time.
Emotions are another way that we experience things, and the same experience can create different emotions in different people.
Senses and emotions are called **'perceptions'** *[per-SEP-shuns]. - noun*
The verb is **'perceive'**.

perceive [per-SEEV] = *to create an opinion based on how you feel about something.*
"I perceive communism as a bad form of government."
"The people in our town perceived [per-SEEVD] the mayor as a good leader."
"Many people have begun perceiving fossil fuels as bad for the environment."
"My perception of Egypt changed when I went there for a holiday." - *'perception' is the noun*

46

We often use adjectives and adverbs when speaking about our perceptions. These give extra information about the subject, object, or action, and gives specific information about our opinion. The examples of the verbs will use a variety of adjectives to show the speakers' perceptions and opinions.

taste [tayst] = *to sense the flavor of food or drinks with our tongue [tung].*
"I think that the chicken curry tastes too salty."
"Her chocolate cake tasted [TAY-sted] delicious [dee-LISH-us]!"
"My friend and I were tasting the food together. She said that it tasted very good, but I thought that it tasted very bad."
"This drink has a slight strawberry taste." - *noun*

smell = *to sense the odors (bad) or scents (good) of things with our nose.*
"I don't want to smell the odor of stinky garbage."
"He smelled [smelld] the wonderful scent of food cooking on the barbeque [BAR-beh-kyoo]."
"I am smelling a terrible stink, like the stench of a dead animal."
"Fresh bread has a lovely, fragrant smell." - *noun*

Nouns used in the category of 'smell':
Good smell: **scent** [sent]**, aroma, bouquet** [boo-KAY]**, fragrance.**
Bad smell: **stink, odor, stench, funk.**

Adjectives used in the category of 'smell':
Good smell: aromatic, **fragrant, scented** [SEN-ted]**, sweet-smelling.**
Bad smell: **stinky, stinking, odorous** [O-dor-us]**, funky, reeking, pungent** [PUN-jent]**.**

sound = *to sense a noise [noyz] with your ears.*
"You sound like a horse when you sneeze."
"That song sounded [SOUN-ded] terrible!"
"Her guitar is sounding better now, because she tuned it."

"In the early morning, the birds make wonderful sounds." - *plural noun*

Nouns used in the category of 'sound':
Good sound nouns: **tempo, cadence** [KAY-denss], **beat.** *(These are used for music)*
Bad sound nouns: **racket, commotion** [kuh-MO-shun], **caterwauling**
[KAT-er-wall-ing],

seem = *something gives a person a perception, or creates an opinion.*
"I seem to have lost my money, because I cannot find it in my bag."
"Her eyes were red, and she seemed [seemd] to be crying."
- *'seeming' is difficult to use as continuous-tense.*
- *'seem' cannot be used as a noun.*

'Seem' is an important verb to understand. It means that the speaker is not sure about how the information will result in a conclusion. The evidence is not 100 percent clear.
Phrases used in the category of 'seem':
Feels like, gives the impression, get the idea that, a feeling in your bones, a sneaking suspicion, gives a perception, have an inkling, have a hunch, have a gut feeling.

feel = *to have a perception, or to create an opinion, based on an event or a physical condition.*
"I feel terrible today. I think that I am getting sick."
"He felt like a fool when his pants fell down." - *past-tense verb changes form*
"We are all feeling happy because we can go to the beach tomorrow."
"The warm sun gives me a nice feeling." - *noun*

appear [uh-PEER] = *to create a perception because of how something looks or seems.*
"With those fancy clothes, you appear to be going to a party."
"My friend appeared [uh-PEERD] to be drunk, but he was only pretending."
"The shadow on the wall is appearing to look like a giant monster's hand."
"He did not get the job because of his dirty appearance." - *noun*
'appear' can also mean *'to arrive', or 'to come into view'.*

look = *to create a perception because of how something appears.*

"You look so happy today!"
"The dark clouds looked [lookt] like rain would come soon."
"He is looking so handsome with his new haircut!"
"The dark color of the room creates a gloomy look." - *noun*

Two ways to pronounce the "TH" sound.

Many words have "th", either at the beginning of the word, in the middle of the word, or at the end of the word. The "th" sound can have two different sounds, depending on the word that you are saying.

The first sound is a blowing sound. It is just air escaping as your tongue touches (or almost touches) your top front teeth. Examples of words that start with the blowing sound are:
thing, think, thought, throw, through and three.
The blowing sound with "th" can also happen in the middle or at the end of a word:
tooth, mathematics, moth, method, enthusiasm, breath, faith, fourth, month, path and cloth.

The other sound is a vibration sound. As the air escapes your mouth, and with your tongue touching your top front teeth, you make a sound with your voice. This combination of blowing air and the sound from your voice creates a vibration where your tongue is touching your teeth, which creates the correct sound for these words:
the, these, those, that, they, their, and though.

The vibration sound with "th" can happen in the middle of a word, but never at the end of a word:
father, mother, further, feather, clothes, together, either and weather.

When some students are speaking English, the "th" words can sound like "d" or "t", which is not correct. Their words and meanings might be understood by the listener, but the sound is not proper.

Instead of **"I think that those three things are there"**, it can sound like **"I tink dat doze tree tings are dare"**.

If your goal is to sound like a native English speaker, you will need to practice the "th" sounds until you say them correctly every time!

Listen to the **English Everyday** video on YouTube for a clear demonstration of the 2 different ways to pronounce "th". Or, find the videos on our website: **EnglishEveryday.info**

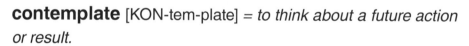

"Think" words.

There are more than one definitions for many of these words but, in this lesson, we are looking at how these verbs are related to 'thinking'.

consider [kon-SID-er] = *to think about something, or think about a future action.*
"I will consider my goals for the future."
"I considered [kon-SID-erd] to the party, but I did not go."
"She is considering what to cook for dinner."
"National health care is a consideration for the government." - *noun*

contemplate [KON-tem-plate] = *to think about a future action or result.*
"I like to contemplate what will happen next year."
"She contemplated [KON-tem-play-ted] where she will work after she finishes university."
"He is contemplating his future opportunities."

"I think that contemplation [kon-tem-PLAY-shun] about your future is important." - noun - the emphasis changes from the verb form!

ponder [PON-der] = to think about something that might be possible in the future.
"Sometimes, I ponder where I will be in ten years."
"She pondered [PON-derd] about when her boyfriend would return home."
"My father is pondering if we can buy a bigger house."
- there is no noun for 'ponder'

*Exercise: Choose two of these verbs: **'consider', 'contemplate', 'ponder'**, and make two sentences. Make one sentence in the the past-tense form, and make one sentence in the present-tense form.*

presume [pree-ZOOM] = to guess that something is true without knowing the facts.
"I presume that you will come to work tomorrow."
"His girlfriend presumed [pree-ZOOMd] that he was at his home, but he was actually at the beach."
"The teacher was presuming that you would attend school today."
"I had a presumption [pree-ZUMP-shun] that you were older than twenty one." - noun

assume [ah-SOOM] = to guess without knowing all the facts.
"He assumes that she is not married."
"She assumed [ah-SOOMD] that he had a good job."
"Your parents are assuming that you will go to university after high school."
"My friend's assumption [ah-SUMP-shun] was not correct." - noun

Exercise: Make a sentence using 'presume', and a sentence using 'assume'. The two words have the same meaning when they are used for 'thinking'. 'Assume' can be also mean 'to take power or responsibility'.

guess [gess] = 1. to believe that something is true, without having clear evidence.
"I guess that I will be eating chicken curry for my dinner."
"Christopher Columbus guessed [gest] that India was on the other side of the Atlantic Ocean."

"She was guessing that a butterfly is a type of bird."
"My guess is that it will rain tomorrow." - *noun*

guess 2. *to estimate an amount, a size, a time or an answer.*
"She guessed that there were about 20 people at the party."
"We all guessed [gest] that the woman was about 30 years old."
"Can you guess which country is the biggest country in the World?"
"I have a guess about how many balls are in that box." - *noun*

believe [bee-LEEV] = *to think that something is true, to have an opinion about something, or to anticipate an action.*
"I believe that she is cooking chicken curry for dinner."
"My friend believed [bee-LEEVD] that I would go to the party."
"I began believing that driving fast is dangerous when I saw an accident."
"His belief [bee-LEEF] is that vampires are real, and not just a story." - *noun*

comprehend [com-pree-HEND] = *to understand, hear, or see clearly.*
"There is too much noise. I cannot comprehend your words."
"She comprehended [com-pree-HEN-ded] everything about geometry."
"He does not comprehend the Japanese language."
"His comprehension [com-pree-HEN-shun] of rocket science is amazing." - *noun*

decide [dee-SIDE] = *to choose one thing after thinking about other options.*
"I cannot decide if I will go to the party or not go."
"She decided [dee-SIDE-ed] to cook chicken curry for dinner."
"He is deciding if he wants to come with us."
"He usually makes good decisions [dee-SIZH-unz]." - *noun*

Exercise: Make two sentences using more than two of these verbs. Use two of the verbs in the same sentence! Try to use a different tense for each verb in each sentence.
Example: "I guess that she has not decided to go with us."

surmise [ser-MIZE] = *to believe that something is true, without having clear evidence. Not a commonly used word!*

"Her home smells like chicken curry, so I surmise that she is cooking chicken curry."

"My friend surmised [ser-MYZD] that I went to the party, but he did not go either."

"The car was destroyed, so I am surmising that the driver was going too fast."

- *the noun "surmise" is rarely used in regular speech*

suppose [sup-POZE] = *1. to believe that something is true, without having clear evidence.*

"I suppose that she will cook chicken curry for dinner."

"He supposed [sup-POZD] that the woman was about 30 years old."

- *the noun "supposition" is rarely used in regular speech*

suppose *2. an invitation to think about, or do, something.*

"Suppose I go to the party tomorrow, will you go too?"

"Do you suppose that you can help me move the table?"

supposed to [sup-POZED to] = *something that you are expected to do.*

"People are supposed to drive at a safe speed, and we are not supposed to drive too fast."

"She was supposed to go to the market yesterday, but she forgot to go."

"Isn't your son supposed to go to school today?"

- *'supposed to' is a phrasal verb*

conclude [kon-KLOOD] = *1. to create a final opinion. No more guessing!*

"I conclude that we will eat chicken curry for dinner."

"He concluded [kon-KLOO-ded] that Russia is the biggest country in the World."

"The doctor is concluding that the boy's sickness is from a spider bite."

"After counting them, the conclusion [kon-KLOO-zhun] is that there are 32 balls in the box." - *noun*

2. (not a 'think' verb) the final part. the end part.

"I would like something sweet to conclude my dinner."

"The teacher concluded the lesson with a science experiment."

"You can ask questions after the conclusion [kon-KLOO-shun] of the lesson." - *noun*

determine [dee-TER-min] = *1. to find an answer using facts and clues.*

"We determine that the meat in the curry is not chicken."

"He determined [dee-TER-mind] that I did not go to the party, because I was not there!"

"The police are determining the cause of the accident."
"The doctor's determination [dee-ter-min-AY-shun] was that the boy's bone was not broken."
- *noun - the emphasis moves to the fourth syllable*

determine 2. *(Not a 'think' verb) the reason that something happens.*
"A student's talent and interest can determine which career they will choose."
"Our body shapes and sizes are determined by the DNA from our parents."
"The direction of the wind will determine which direction the tree will fall."
- *'determination' is difficult to use as a noun in this way*

Exercise: *Think about a different way to use either* **'conclude'** *or* **'determine'.**
Then, speak your sentence out loud. Repeat the sentence three times.

intend [in-TEND] = *to plan. To have a purpose.*
"I intend to go to university when I finish high school."
"She intended [in-TEN-ded] to go to the party, but she did not go."
"Cars are intended to be driven at safe speeds."
"Her intention [in-TEN-shun] was to make a new dress." - *noun*

make up your mind = *to make a choice. To decide.*
"I couldn't make up my mind whether to walk to school or go to school on the bus."
"She finally made up her mind to buy the red hat, but she liked the blue hat too."
"When we all make up our minds about what we want to eat, we can cook it."
"The students made up their minds to study in groups, instead of individually."

figure out = *to understand the reason why.*
"I couldn't figure out why she used goat meat instead of chicken meat."
"My friends figured out that I was not at the party, because they didn't see me there!"
"People should figure out that driving fast is not safe."
"She used a calculator to figure out that 288 divided by 12 equals 24."

Creative thinking.

imagine [im-AJ-in] = *to create an idea in your mind. To think of an image or a design.*
"Can you imagine a world without war?"
"The boy imagined [im-AJ-ind] that he was a pirate."
"She is imagining a new design for a dress."
"Use your imagination [ih-mah-jin-AY-shun] to create a story." - *noun - emphasis changes*

picture [PICK-chur] = *to create or imagine. To think of an image or a design.*
"Try to picture what your brother would look like if he was a girl."
"In his mind, he pictured [PICK-churd] a red sky, a purple sea, and yellow mountains."
"I am picturing my mother with a beard."
"He created a mental picture of a big dragon." - *noun*

visualize [VIZH-yoo-al-ize] = *to create an image or a design by using a picture, or by using your imagination. When we visualize, we can have a better idea of the final result.*
"I am trying to visualize your description of the city."
"As they talked about the project, they visualized [VIZH-yoo-al-aizd] the details of their plan."
"We are visualizing the results of our success [suk-SESS]."
"A plan is not easy to imagine without something visual [VIZH-yoo-al]." - *the noun 'visual' means 'something that you can see with your eyes'. It is different that imagining.*

fantasize [FAN-ta-size] = *to create or imagine a story.*
"I like to fantasize that I am fighting with a dragon."
"She fantasized [FAN-ta-syzd] about marrying a prince."
"I am fantasizing about my holiday next month. Maybe I will go to the beach."
"My fantasy is to be rich and famous." - *noun*

Exercise: *Choose three of these verbs, and create three sentences that give examples of* **'imagining'**, **'picturing'**, **'visualizing'** *or* **'fantasizing'**. *Past-tense might be the easiest way.*

concentrate [KON-sen-trayt] = *to focus your thoughts, thinking about only one thing.*
"If I concentrate on physics, I can learn everything quickly."
"Last year, she concentrated [KON-sen-tray-ted] on playing guitar."

"Today our class is concentrating on learning verbs and adverbs."
"Focus your concentration [kon-sen-TRAY-shun] on the correct pronunciation." - *noun - changes emphasis*

expect [eks-PECT] = *to think that something will happen in the future.*
"I expect that it will be very hot this summer."
"We expected [eks-PEC-ted] our friend to come with us, but she did not come."
"My father is expecting that his boss will give him a higher salary."
"Sometimes, you can be disappointed if your expectation [eks-pekt-TAY-shun] is too ambitious." - *noun - emphasis changes to the third syllable*

anticipate [an-TISS-ah-payt] = *to believe that something will happen before it happens.*
"I anticipate that my wife will arrive at 4 o'clock today."
"Before the concert, we anticipated [an-TISS-ah-pay-ted] that the crowd would be small."
"She is anticipating a new dress for her birthday gift."
"We were filled with a feeling of anticipation [an-tiss-ah-PAY-shun]." - *noun - emphasis changes to the third syllable*

Exercise: *Make one sentence using either* **'concentrate'**, **'expect'**, *or* **'anticipate'**.

reason [REE-zun] = *to create an opinion or a result by thinking about the evidence.*
"We can see apples in the bag, so we can reason that the bag is full of apples."
"She reasoned [REE-zund] that he loved her because he gave her a gold bracelet."
"Inventors create successful ideas by reasoning what people need."
"If I do not have a good reason to go, I will not go anywhere." - *noun*

reckon [REK-un] = *to create an opinion or a result by thinking about the evidence. Can be used the same way as 'reason'. 'Reckon' also means to calculate or estimate.*
"I reckon that there are about 150 people at this party."
"She reckoned [REK-und] that he would return in 30 minutes."
"The driver is reckoning that it will take 2 hours to reach our destination."
"According to my reckoning, the car should cost about 8,000 dollars." – *gerund noun*

figure [FIG-yur] = *to think that something is true because of an opinion, experience or evidence. Or, to calculate or estimate.*

"I figure that I have about 2,000 dollars in my bank account."

"Because of the distance, she figured [FIG-yurd] that it takes 3 hours to drive to Bangkok."

"He is figuring that in 6 months, he will be finished with his project."

"The figures for the price estimate are too high." - *noun*

deem = *a conclusion based on opinion or evidence.*

"We deem that investing in your business is a good idea."

"My boss deemed [deemd] that I was ready for a higher salary."

"She is deeming that her boyfriend can be trusted with her young sister."

-*'deem' does not have a noun*

Exercise: *Use the verb* **'figure'** *in a sentence, then say it out loud three times.*

estimate [EH-stih-mate] = *to guess (based on evidence) about how much time, resources, or money will be needed. Also, guess about size, age, quantity, or another countable quality.*

"I estimate a 10-hour bus ride from Bogotá, Columbia to Quito, Ecuador."

"She estimated [EH-stih-may-ted] that I was 30 years old."

"She is estimating that 650 meters of electrical wire will be needed."

"The estimate [ESS-tih-met] for the new stadium is 10 million dollars." - *noun - pay attention, because the pronunciation changes!*

Phrases used for estimating: **give a ballpark figure, a rough estimation, a rough estimate, a guesstimate.**

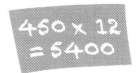

calculate [KAL-kyoo-late] = *to find an amount, or a total number, using mathematics.*

"We need to calculate how much money we will spend on the project."

"She calculated [KAL-kyoo-lay-ted] that 35 people would come to the party."

"Calculating expenses is important for a business."

"My calculation [kal-kyoo-LAY-shun] is 60,000 dollars to build the house." - *the pronunciation changes for the noun!*

Other ways to say 'estimate' and 'calculate' are: **figure out, figure it out, make sense of it, do the math, run the numbers.**

Exercises:
• *Calculate how many boxes you will need if you have 144 eggs, and only 12 eggs can fit in each box.*

• *Estimate how many days you need to walk before you reach your goal. You will walk at around 3 miles per hour, and the total distance is about 600 miles. Each day, you will walk for an average of 10 hours.*

• *Calculate the amount of days between November 14 of this year, and April 27 of next year.*

regard [ree-GARD] = *your opinion about something or somebody.*
"I regard him as a trusted friend."
"We all regarded [ree-GAR-ded] our chemistry teacher as the best teacher in the school."
"You should be regarding homework as a benefit for your future."
"The staff should have high regard for our customers." - *noun*

reflect [ree-FLEKT] = *to remember a past event or a past emotion.*
"I like to reflect about my childhood."
"My father reflected [ree-FLEK-ted] about when he was a boy."
"She is reflecting about her sadness when her grandmother died."
"Our reflections [ree-FLEK-shuns] about the past can give us guidance for our future." - *noun*

meditate [MED-ih-tate] = *to find peace and quiet by relaxing your mind.*
"Many people meditate in order to to find new ideas."
"As I meditated [MED-ih-tay-ted], I thought of a better way to teach my children math."
"She is meditating. Please be quiet."
"Meditation [med-ih-TAY-shun] calms my mind and relieves my stress." - *noun - pay attention, because the emphasis changes!*

contemplate [KON-tem-plate] = *to think about something before an action.*
"I will contemplate my various career options before I choose."
"My friend contemplated [KON-tem-play-ted] quitting school, but he did not quit."
"The United Nations is contemplating economic sanctions."
"Contemplation [kon-tem-PLAY-shun] is the first step towards a smart plan." - *noun - emphasis changes to the third syllable.*

brainstorm [BRAIN-storm] = *to create as many ideas as you can to solve a problem or find an answer.*
"We can brainstorm about what to do to build our business."
"She brainstormed [BRAIN-stormd] until midnight about how to design the house."
"They are brainstorming a new idea for a website."
"Many great ideas are created by brainstorming." - *gerund*

Common words and phrases used for 'contemplate': **scrutinize, consider, thoughtful observation, think about it, mull it over, give some thought to it.**

*Exercise: Use the word **'contemplate'** in a sentence. Think about something that YOU plan to do in the future.*

Will do, want to do, like to do and need to do.

able (use a long 'a' sound) [AYE-bul] - *adjective = can do something, have the skill.*
"Are you able to speak English?"
"She is an able worker, and she has many skills."
"Using irrigation, people are able to grow crops in the desert."

able is a very important word to know, because it is used as a prefix (at the beginning) and a suffix (at the end) of many other words. Adding **'able'** to a word changes verbs and nouns into adjectives or adverbs.

59

The pronunciation changes when used as a suffix. The long 'A' in 'able' becomes a short 'A' sound (ah). Here are some examples: **comfortable** [KUM-fort-ah-bul], **reasonable** [REE-zon-ah-bul], **unbreakable** [un-BRAKE-ah-bul].

Let's look at 'able' used as different forms of grammar.

ability (use a short 'a' sound) [ah-BIL-ih-tee] - *noun = skill or opportunity to do something.*
"She has the ability to play guitar and sing at the same time."
"The country of Ukraine had the ability to separate from the Soviet Union in 1991."

capable (short 'a' sound for -able) [KAPE-ah-bul] - *adjective = can do something, to have the skill for a specific job.*
"Some animals are capable of jumping 2 meters high."
"A submarine is capable of staying underwater for three months."
"In the fifteenth century, sailing ships were capable of traveling for thousands of miles."

capability (short 'a' sound) [kape-ah-BIL-it-ee] - *noun = can do something, have the skill.*
"Many people don't reach the limits of their capabilities."
"The factory has the capability to make 800 refrigerators per day."
"At least 29 countries in the world have nuclear capability."

Common phrases that have similar meanings to 'able', 'ability' and 'capable':
can do, has the skills, fit to, in a position to, up to (a limit), **has the potential for, has the means to.**

Exercise: Using the adjective 'capable', create three sentences. Choose from these words for the subject or object nouns: airplane, people, volcano, temperature, height, future, history, speed, man, woman.

Can we do it?

allow [ah-LAU] = *to let something happen, or give a chance to do something.*
"I will allow my son to go to the party."
"The umbrella allowed [ah-LOUD] me to stay dry in the rainstorm."
"Technology is allowing [ah-LAU-ing] many people to work at their homes."
"An allowance [ah-LAU-ants] is an amount of money given to someone or to a project." - *noun*

permit [per-MIT] = *to allow something to happen.*
"I will permit you to go with your friends if you clean the house first."
"He was permitted [per-MIT-ted] to go home from school early."
"The hole in the roof is permitting water to fall into the house."
"The teacher gave the students permission [per-MISH-un] to sing a popular song." - *noun*

*Exercise: Write two sentences using **'allow'** and **'permit'**. Use examples about yourself. What activities or actions are NOT allowed and permitted for you?*

Do we want to do it?

want and **desire** [dee-ZIRE] = *want to do something. Or, want to have something.*
"I can take care of your wants and desires." - *nouns*
"He has the desire to attend the university." - *noun*
"We desire new tables and chairs for the students." - *verb*
"I will not go to the market because I have no desire to go." - *'desire' is used as a noun*
"I do not want to go." - *'want' is a present-tense verb, 'to go' is an infinitive verb*

aspire [ah-SPIRE] = *hope to be better, want to reach a goal.*
"I aspire to be a violin player in the orchestra."
"When the boy was younger, he aspired [ah-SPYRD] to be a football player."
"She is an aspiring actress." - *adjective*
"His mother is sad because her son has no aspiration for the future." - *noun*

Common phrases that have similar meanings to want, desire, and aspire: **would like, dream about, wish for, yearn for, have your heart set on, set your sights on.**

Exercise: Use the verb 'desire', and the phrasal verb 'aspire to be', and create three sentences. Think about what YOU want for yourself!

wish = *to want something that might not be easy to get.*
"I wish the rain would stop. It is raining too much!"
"We wished [wisht] we could go to visit our grandmother."
"He is wishing that she didn't have a boyfriend already."
"Buying a bigger house is one of her wishes." - *plural noun*

dream = *things that people think about when they sleep, or things that people imagine when they are awake.*
"I dream about attending the university in London."
She dreamt [drempt] about flying with the birds." - *past-tense changes form*
"She dreamed [dreemd] about flying with the birds." - *past-tense*
'dreamt' and 'dreamed' are both correct ways to use this verb in past-tense
"Last night, I had a dream that I could walk on the clouds." - *noun*

hope = *good things that people wish will happen.*
"I hope that I will be successful in the future."
"She hoped [hoapt] the rain would stop before she went to school."
"We are all hoping for peace in the world."
"Our hope is that we can get new books for the library." - *noun*

Common phrases that have similar meanings to 'wish', 'dream' and 'hope': **would like, have a chance, yearn for, have your heart set on, set your sights on.**

Exercise: Make a sentence, and use all three words. Talk about the wishes, dreams and hopes that YOU have!

The adjective 'specific' is important to understand!

specific [speh-SIF-ik] = *a clear definition or message. 'specific' directs the focus to the exact thing, and not other things that are similar.*

"I want to buy a shirt, but not any shirt. I want a red shirt with black stripes, not a blue shirt with green stripes." - *this is a specific message.*

"She likes to study biology, but she does not like her biology teacher.
She would like to continue studying biology, but she wants a different teacher."
- *the student does not like the **specific** teacher. She wants to study biology with a different teacher, but she is **not specific** about which teacher she wants.*

"My friend said that he wants a new phone. I gave my friend a new Sony phone, and he was not happy.
I asked him why he was not happy, and my friend said that he wanted a *Samsung* phone, not a *Sony* phone!"
-*he was **not specific** about the brand when he requested a new phone.*

Other adjectives that are similar to 'specific': **precise, exact, definite, certain, focused, clear-cut, specialized, direct, sure, positive.**

'**specific**' means *an exact thing.*
The opposite adjectives of '**specific**' are '**general**' and '**vague**'.

general [JEN-er-al] = *not an exact definition or message. 'General' can include many things in a group or a category.*

vague [vayg] = *not clear or definite. Difficult to recognize or understand.*

Other adjectives that are similar to 'general' : **common, ordinary, regular, nonspecific, popular, universal, overall, assorted, unspecialized, typical, standard, routine, rough.**

Other adjectives that are similar to 'vague': **obscure, imprecise, unfocused, arbitrary, nonspecific, sketchy, foggy, ambiguous, unclear.**

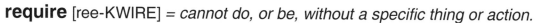

Do we need to do it? Do we need to have it?

need = *cannot do, or be, without a specific thing or action.*
"People need food to survive."
"We needed [NEE-ded] water for the garden"
"Will you be needing any more supplies?"
"Do you have a need for more books?" - *noun*

require [ree-KWIRE] = *cannot do, or be, without a specific thing or action.*
"The people in the village require water to drink and grow their gardens."
"All students were required [ree-KWYRd] to wear uniforms to school."
"The boss is requiring everyone to use safety equipment."
"You cannot graduate if you have not passed all of the required courses." - *adjective*

Common words and phrases that have similar meanings to need and require:
necessary, essential, have to, need to, it's needed, mandatory, must have, it is a prerequisite, can't do without.

*Exercise: Use the verb '**need**' in two sentences, using two different verb tenses. Use the adjective '**required**' in two sentences, using at least two different subject nouns.*

When we need an opinion.

An opinion [o-PIN-yun] is what someone 'thinks' about something. Different people have different opinions about what they like and do not like. An opinion is not a 'fact', an opinion is the result of how people think and feel about things.

suggest [sug-JEST] = *to offer an idea.*
"All of my friends suggest that I wear a helmet when I ride a motorcycle."
"My teacher suggested [sug-JEST-ed] studying more If I want to attend university."
"Her mother is suggesting that she wears a jacket when she goes outside."
"A good suggestion [sug-JEST-chun] can save your life sometimes!" - *noun*

advise [ad-VIZE] = *to offer an idea based on experience or opinion.*
"My father will advise me about how to invest money."
"The doctor advised [ad-VYZD] me to eat a lot of vegetables."
"A mother should be advising her daughter about many things."
"My teacher's advice [ad-VICE] showed me the best ways to study and learn." - *noun*

recommend [REK-om-END] = *to offer an idea based on experience.*
"I recommend that you do what your parents tell you to do."
"The man recommended [REK-om-EN-ded] going a different direction."
"She is recommending to add more salt to the soup."
"I agreed with his recommendation [REK-om-en-DAY-shun] about the restaurant." - *noun*

*Exercise: Make one sentence using '**suggest**'. You can use any verb tense that you like. Then, use the same sentence and replace '**suggest**' with '**advise**' and '**recommend**'. Use the same verb tense for all three sentences.*

imply [im-PLY] = *to suggest that something is true, something will happen, or something has happened, without saying the words directly.*
"How do you imply that you don't have any money? You can shake your head 'no' and show your empty hands."

"She implied [im-PLYD] that she would go to the market today, but she did not say when."

"When you make a sad face, you are implying that you are not having fun."

"The water on the floor is an implication [im-plih-KAY-shun] that a pipe is broken." - *noun*

insinuate [in-SIN-yoo-ate] = *to suggest that something is true, something will happen, or something has happened, without saying the words directly. Same as 'imply'.*

"I will not insinuate that my friend took the money. I don't think that he would do that."

"Our teacher insinuated [in-SIN-yoo-ate-ed] that no students passed the chemistry test."

"The dark clouds are insinuating that rain will come soon."

"An insinuation [in-sin-yoo-AY-shun] is not the same as evidence." - *noun*

*-the noun '**allegation**' is similar to the noun 'insinuation'.*

infer [in-FURR] = *to decide or conclude that something is true, or something will happen, or has happened, because of some kind of evidence.*

"You can infer that the weather will be hot tomorrow because the weather is hot today."

"All of the apples in this box are rotten, so we inferred [in-FURD] that the apples in all of the other boxes are rotten too."

"The news story is inferring that the war in Afghanistan will continue for a long time."

"I believe the inference [IN-fer-ents] that the tsunami was caused by an earthquake."- *noun*

pretend [pree-TEND] = *to make motions, actions, or words to appear that something is real or true, but it is not real or true. 'Pretend' is similar to 'fake' (see page 76).*

"I like to pretend that I can play guitar, but I don't even have a guitar!"

"She pretended [pree-TEN-ded] to be crying, but she was not really crying."

"The boys are pretending that they are soldiers, and using bananas as guns."

"He is singing, and using a bottle as a pretend microphone." - *adjective*

hint = *to give a little bit of information to direct an answer or a solution.*

"I will hint that I know the answer by writing the first letter of the word."

"My mother hinted [HIN-ted] that she would give me a new bicycle for my birthday."

"My friend is hinting that he wants to play football by pretending to kick a ball."

"The new president gave us many hints about his future economic policies." - *plural noun*

Exercise: *Make two sentences using two of these verbs: 'imply', 'insinuate', 'pretend' or 'hint'. Use your own experience to create the sentences.*

When we feel confident.

promise [PROH-miss] = *a person says that they will definitely do something.*
"The children promise that they will clean the house tomorrow."
"She promised [PROM-ist] her boss that she would come to work on Saturday."
"I am promising myself that I will go to sleep early tonight."
"He said he would come, but he did not come. He broke his promise." - *noun*

assure [ah-SHOOR] = *to promise, to make someone feel sure that the story is true.*
"I assure you that the boat is safe. It will not sink in the river."
"The shopkeeper assured [ah-SHOORD] me that the tool would work well."
"The father is assuring his son that there is not a monster under the bed."
"His father's assurance [ah-SHOO-rance] made him feel safe." - *noun*

guarantee [gair-an-TEE] = *to promise, or give total assurance.*
"I can guarantee that I will return tomorrow."
"The car is guaranteed [gair-an-TEED] for two years."
"He is guaranteeing [gair-an-TEE-ing] to fix the machine if it breaks."
"The banks have a guarantee that your money is safe." - *noun*

commit [kuh-MITT] = *promise money, time, or effort for a project or an action.*
"I don't want to commit all of my money to my business."
"She committed [kuh-MIT-ted] to teach English in Vietnam for three years.
"He is committing five hours per day to the project."
"Her boss is very impressed with he commitment [kuh-MIT-ment] to her job." - *noun*

dedicate [DED-ih-kate] = *to give money, time, or effort for a project or an action.*
"I will dedicate my extra time to teach the kids."
"This money is dedicated [DED-ih-kate-ed] to our family holiday."
"We are dedicating every Friday morning to clean the litter in the town."
"His dedication [ded-ih-KAY-shun] to his children's education takes most of his time." - *noun*

Other words and phrases that are similar to 'commit' and 'dedicate':
allocate, assign, devote, earmark, set aside for.

pledge [plej], **vow** and **swear** [sware] = *to make a promise.*
"I pledge to follow the rules of the school."
"She vowed [vowd] to take care of her sick husband."
"They all swore [swore] to keep the secret." - *past-tense verb changes form*
"I can trust him because of his pledge to be honest." - *noun*

Exercise: Use three of the verbs in present-tense sentences, then read the sentences out loud. Use your own experience for your subjects!

We can do it!

motivate [MOTE-eh-vate] = *to create interest for an action or a positive change.*
"What will motivate you to learn English?"
"The father motivated [MOTE-eh-vay-ted] his son to study by giving him a video game if he gets good grades in school."
"Our boss is motivating us to perform better by offering us more holiday time."
"Compliments about her fashion design gave her motivation [mote-e-VAY-shun] to create more new styles." - *noun - changes emphasis!*

Common phrases that have similar meanings to motivate and motivation:
light a fire, get stimulated, the carrot on a stick, reach the goal, the prize, burning desire.

Exercise: Discuss what motivates YOU. If you are in a group, everyone can talk about their motivation.

encourage [en-KUR-aj] = *to give positive support and confidence.*
"You should encourage children to study and learn, not just play with their friends."
"Our teacher encouraged [en-KUR-ajd] us to attend university after we finish high school."
"My parents' support is encouraging me to be a better student."
"Encouragement [en-KUR-aj-ment] creates motivation." - *noun*

Common phrases that have similar meanings to 'encourage' and 'encouragement':
give support, put ideas in your head, cheer up, spur on, give a shot in the arm, "you can do it!".

suggest [sug-JEST] = *to give a good idea, or a different way to do something.*
"I want to suggest a better way to fix the machine."
"Her friend suggested [sug-JEST-ed] that finding a job was more important than going to school."
"The teacher is suggesting that writing with a pencil is better than writing with a pen."
"I like your suggestion [sug-JEST-chun], but I like my way better." - *noun*

advise [ad-VIZE] = to give a good idea based on a person's past experience.
"Can you advise me about which career I should choose?"
"He advised [ad-VYZD] me about the best way to cook chicken."
"When you are advising your children, think about your own experiences."
"My father always gave me the best advice." [ad-VICE] - *noun - changes pronunciation*

recommend [REK-om-END] = *to suggest the best thing or the best course of action, or to give a good review about a person or a thing.*
"Could you recommend the most delicious food in this restaurant?"
"My teacher recommended [REK-om-EN-ded] me for the scholarship."
"His recommendation is that I go to my house now, to avoid the rain." - *noun*

Words and phrases that are commonly used for 'suggest', 'advise' and 'recommend' are: **support, endorse, speak well of, speak favorably about.**

Exercise: Think about a good suggestion, good advice, or a recommendation that someone gave to you. Then, write a short story about it.

Don't do it!

incite [in-SITE] = *to create anger or bad behavior with words or an action.*
"We expect that the argument will incite him to hurt someone."
"The fight on the football field incited [in-SITE-ed] the spectators to fight."
"Higher taxes are inciting the citizens to protest."
- *no noun for 'incite'*

provoke [pro-VOKE] = *to create anger, encourage anger, or make angrier.*
"I don't want to provoke him. He is already angry."
"When the man provoked [pro-VOAKT] him, the fight started."
"She is provoking her brother by playing with his toys."
"A snake will not attack someone without provocation." [proh-vo-KAY-shun]- *noun*

Common phrases that have similar meanings to '**incite**' and '**provoke**': **stir up, rile up, fan the flames, fuel the fire, egg on, put bad ideas in your head, spur on, prod, spark off.**

Exercise: Think about something that has provoked or incited you. What makes you angry?

exaggerate [eg-ZAD-jur-ate] = *to talk about something in a way that makes something seem bigger, better, or more, than it actually is.*
"She exaggerates about how many friends she has."
"Donald Trump exaggerated [eg-ZAD-jur-ate-ed] about how many people attended his inauguration ceremony."
"He says that he is the strongest man in the world, but he is exaggerating."
"To say that he is a rich man is an exaggeration." [eg-zad-jur-A-shun] - *noun*

70

Words commonly used as exaggerations include: **always, constantly, forever, incessantly, non-stop, unending, persistently, endlessly, perpetually, eternally, forever, all the time, repeatedly, 24-7 (24 hours a day, and 7 days a week).**

These are commonly used words and, even though they are not always accurate, they are part of everyday English!

Keep going!

continue [kon-TINN-yoo] = *to keep doing something, to stay the same, or to start again.*

"After ten years, she continues to work at the bank."

"We continued [kon-TIN-yood] walking after a short break to relax."

"I plan on continuing my education for many more years."

"My daughter is continually looking at Facebook." - *adverb*

proceed [pro-SEED] = *to continue doing something after stopping. To go forward.*

"You can proceed with your homework after you eat dinner."

"The man stopped to ask directions, then he proceeded [pro-SEE-ded] walking."

"The train is proceeding to New York after it stops in Boston."

"Doctors follow the procedures [pro-SEED-jurz] that they learned in medical school."
- plural noun

advance [ad-VANTS] = *to move forward, to make progress.*

"As technology advances, our life becomes easier, but more complicated."

"The soldiers advanced [ad-VANST] their position to attack the city."

"Ancient Greece was an advanced [ad-VANST] society 2600 years ago. They focused on philosophy, architecture, astronomy, democracy, medicine and the arts." - *'advanced' is used as an adjective*

"Scientific research has created many advances [ad-VANTS-es] for our health." - *plural noun*

progress [pro-GRESS] = *to move forward, to improve, to go in the desired direction.*

"Medical science will progress as knowledge of the human body progresses."

"The speed of computer microchips has progressed [pro-GREST] in the past 5 years."

"The ship is progressing through the foggy weather."
"We are making progress [PRAW-gress] every day." - *pay attention to the different syllable emphasis when used as a noun!*

Exercise: Create two sentences, one with the verb 'progress', and one with the noun 'progress'. Speak the two sentences, paying attention to the pronunciation of the words. Remember, the emphasis changes!

persevere [pur-seh-VEER] = *to continue a difficult action, and not quit.*
"Even though it is difficult, we will persevere with our learning."
"The family persevered [per-seh-VEERD] through the long, cold winter, although they had barely enough food to survive."
"The president is persevering with his effort for tax reform."
"My teacher had amazing perseverance [per-seh-VEER-ants] - *noun*

Common phrases for "persevere": **hang on, carry on, hold on, press on, press ahead, keep going, stick with it, stick to it, hang in there, plug away, don't give up, don't quit, stand your ground, be tenacious, hammer away, stop at nothing, don't take 'no' for an answer.**

Exercise: Using the following events, create sentences using these verbs. You can change the verb tenses if you want to: **continue, proceed, advance.**

Advanced Exercise: Use four of the phrases that mean 'to persevere' and create four sentences. Be creative, and use examples about yourself!

We did it!

reward [ree-WOARD] = *to receive a fair result for your actions.*
"The boss will reward the best workers with extra money."
"For his good grades in school, the boy was rewarded [ree-WOARD-ed] with a new bicycle."
"My school will be rewarding the best student with a scholarship to the university."

"His reward for returning the lost money was one hundred dollars." - *noun*

Other words and phrases in the category of 'incentive' and 'reward':
payoff, return on investment, outcome, "what's in it for me?", result.

Exercise: Using the following events, create sentences using these verbs. You can change the verb tenses if you want to: **continue, proceed, advance, progress, persevere.**

It is not always good.

cause [kawz] = *to make something bad happen.*
"Drinking dirty water will cause people to be sick."
"The flat tire caused [kawzd] the bus to crash."
"The boys are in trouble because they were causing problems in school."
"My girlfriend is the cause of my broken heart." - *noun*
Cause *is an important word to understand. It is similar to the conjunction "because", which means "for the reason that..." A person, a thing or an action will 'cause' a result. The result cannot happen without the thing or action that 'caused' it.*

punish [PUN-ish] = *to give a penalty because of bad behavior or a wrong action.*
"My mother will punish me if I do not clean the house today."
"The two brothers were punished [PUN-isht] because they broke a chair."
"The father is punishing his son by taking the boys telephone away for one week."
"The punishment for driving drunk is six months in the jail." - *noun*

suffer [SUFF-er] = *to live with pain, sickness or something bad.*
"I suffer with migraine headaches almost every day."
"He has suffered [SUFF-erd] with malaria for one week."
"My family is suffering the loss of my grandfather."
"It makes me sad to see other people suffering." - *gerund noun*

tolerate [TOL-er-ate] = *to let something happen that you don't like or enjoy.*

"I don't like it, but I will tolerate the smoke from my neighbor's fire."
"My parents tolerated [TOL-er-ate-ed] my bad study habits."
"Her leg is injured badly, but she is tolerating the pain."
"Toleration [tol-er-AYE-shun] of pollution [poh-LOO-shun] is not good for our society."-*noun*

endure [en-DYUR or en-DYOOR] = *to suffer, tolerate, or not break, and continue to be useful.*
"I cannot endure a lot of pain. It makes me cry and scream."
"He endured [en-DYOORD] 10 years in prison."
"The bridge is enduring the earthquake. It has not fallen down yet."
"The car is 60 years old, and it still works. It has great endurance [en-DYOOR-ants]." - *noun*

stand and **withstand** = *(not the same definition as 'standing up')* to endure or tolerate an action.
"I can stand the noise, but I can't stand the smell!"
"The old house withstood the storm." - *past-tense verb changes form.*
"The soldiers are withstanding the attack by the enemy army."
"I don't know how she is standing our new teacher. I think he is so boring!"
"We need to take a stand against pollution [poh-LOO-shun] from the factory." - *noun*

Phrases that are used for words in this category: **put up with, live with, deal with, can't face it, can't take any longer, cannot bear any longer, can't stomach it.**

Exercise: Think about a time when you had to tolerate or endure something that you did not enjoy. Write a short story about that time, and use as many of these verbs as you can.

Verbs we use for looking at things.

gaze = *to look at something interesting or peaceful.*
"I like to gaze at the lake. It gives me a nice feeling."

"She gazed [gayzd] at the beautiful sunset."
"The mother is gazing at her cute baby."
"His long gaze at the TV made me think that he was sleeping." - *noun*

view = *to look at something.*
"I would like to view the popular places in the city."
"As she viewed [viewd] the mountains, she saw an eagle flying."
"The boss is viewing the accounting books."
"The view of the garbage dump gives me a bad feeling." - *noun*

glance [glants] = *to look at something for a short moment.*
"One glance of the dead dog is all you need to see."
"I glanced [glanst] at the river for a moment, then I continued driving."
"As she was glancing at the newspaper, she saw a photo of her father."
"One glance, and I knew she would be my wife someday." - *noun*

glimpse [glimps] = *able to see something for only a short moment.*
"I could only glimpse my friend in the crowd of people."
"She quickly glimpsed [glimpst] the red hat he was wearing before he disappeared."
"We kept glimpsing the deer as it ran through the forest."
"They caught a glimpse of the ocean before the train entered the tunnel." - *noun*

spot = *to see a specific thing that might be difficult to see.*
"Can you spot the owl in that tree?"
"He spotted [SPOT-ed] his eyeglasses under the table."
"She is spotting a lot of fossils in the rocks."
"Her best spot of the day was the dinosaur tooth fossil." - *noun*

stare = *to look at something directly for a long time.*
"Sometimes, I stare at the clouds for many hours."
"As she stared [staird] at me, I stared back at her."
"The children are staring at the show on the TV."
"That man's stare is making me feel scared." - *noun*

Exercise: Choose three 'looking at' verbs, and build three sentences. Then, speak the sentences out loud.

Seeing the differences and similarities.

identify [eye-DENT-ih-fye] = *to recognize what something is, or to understand a subject.*

"Can someone identify what animal made these footprints?"

"The police identified [eye-DENT-ih-fyd] the murderer, but they have not caught him yet."

"The scientists are identifying new species of animals in Madagascar."

"He could not go onto the airplane because he did not have an identification (ID) card." - *adjective*

recognize [REK-ug-nize] = *to remember something you have experienced before.*

To identify something because you remember it. To understand the difference between two things.

"We could not recognize him because he was wearing a hat and dark glasses."

"I recognized [REK-ug-nyzd] my first-grade teacher at the party."

"Until she tasted them, she was not recognizing the difference between salt and sugar."

"The best student in the school did not receive any special recognition [rek-ug-NISH-un]."

-the noun 'recognition' means that someone is recognized for their ability

Exercise: Choose either 'identify' or 'recognize' and make a sentence using present tense.

compare [kom-PAIR] = *to see what is different and what is the same.*

"Students like to compare their test grades to see who is the smartest."

"Compared [kom-PAIRD] to his brother, he is fat. Compared to his sister, he is slender."

"I am comparing the prices of fruit at the market because I want the lowest price."

"There are not many comparisons [kom-PAIR-iss-unz] between a fish and an elephant." - *noun*

resemble [ree-ZEM-bul] = *to look similar to another thing or another person.*

"The shape of a horse resembles the shape of a zebra."

"The two brothers resembled [ree-ZEM-buld] each other, but the older brother was taller."

76

- *'resembling' is not commonly used in continuous tense*
"There is a resemblance [ree-ZEM-bul-unts] between humans and chimpanzees" - *noun*

equate [ee-KWATE] = *to compare and understand what things are the same.*
"Some people can equate working and fun. Other people think that working is not fun."
"German cars are equated [ee-KWATE-ed] with high quality."
"Our teacher is equating Italian language and Latin language. There are similar words."
"She studied the equations [ee-KWAY-zhun] of philosophy and psychology." - *plural noun*

differentiate [diff-er-EN-chee-ate] = *to compare and see what is different.*
"We can differentiate people by looking at their fingerprints."
"He differentiated [diff-er-EN-chee-ate-ed] the diamonds by size, and separated the biggest ones from the smallest ones."
"The football coach is differentiating [diff-er-EN-chee-ate-ing] the best players to choose for the championship game."
-no noun for 'differentiate'

distinguish [de-STING-gwish] = *to compare and see what is different, or what can be recognized because of the differences.*
"It is difficult to distinguish the difference between the twin sisters."
"Reptiles are distinguished [de-STING-gwisht] from mammals by being cold-blooded."
"Tomorrow, my teacher will be distinguishing the differences between the planets."
"What are the distinctions [de-STINK-shuns] between African and Asian elephants?" - *noun*

Words and phrases for looking at differences and similarities: **tell apart, see the difference between, tell the difference between, discern** [dy-SERN]**, set apart,**

*Exercise: Choose two of these **'comparing'** verbs, and use them in the past tense. Write two sentences, and then speak the sentences out loud.*

specify [SPESS-ih-fy] = *to identify exactly, or to say the exact details.*
"Our teacher will specify which lessons will be included in the test."
"He specified [SPESS-ih-fyd] which 5 books we will read this semester."

"We will build the robot according to the specifications (the plans). - *noun*
"He needs a specific [speh-SIF-ik] part so that he can repair his car."-*adjective-changes emphasis to the second syllable*

perceive [per-SEEV] (also on page 46) = *to see and recognize something, based on opinion.*
"The doctor could not perceive any bacteria in the blood sample."
"The teacher perceived [per-SEEVD] the student as a lazy boy because he was sleeping."
"I was perceiving the shadow on the wall as monster's hand."
"We have opinions about people based on our perception [per-SEP-shun]." - *noun*

Exercise: *Use the verbs '**specify**' or '**perceive**' and make two sentences, one sentence in present tense, and one sentence in past continuous tense.*

Verbs for actions we do not like.

lie [lye] = *to say things that are not true.*
"Did you lie to your mother about finishing your homework?"
"He lied [lyd] to his girlfriend, and now she is angry."
"If you don't stop lying, nobody will believe anything you say!"
"When she said that her friend took the money, that was a lie." - *noun*

deceive [dee-SEEV] = *to make someone believe things that are not true, or create an action that someone believes, but it is not real.*
"I will deceive my sister by wearing a monster costume and making scary sounds."
"The rubber snake deceived [dee-SEEVD] the young boy. He thought that it was a real snake."
"Some people say that the government is always deceiving the citizens of the country."
"His deception [dee-SEP-shun] made us feel angry and embarrassed." - *noun*

trick = *to make someone believe things that are not true, or create an action that someone believes, but it is not real.*
"He wanted to trick me into believing his story, because he wanted me to support him."
"My older brother tricked [trikt] me into going outside. He said he saw an elephant."

"She is tricking her friend into eating spicy food. She said it was not spicy at all."
"He deceived me with his amazing magic trick." - *noun*

act = *to behave in a way that is not a person's true feeling, or not a true story.*
"I will act like my leg is hurt, and my brother will have to do all the work."
"He acted [AK-ted] like he was happy, but he was sad."
"She is crying and screaming and acting like a little baby."
"He said that he was sick, but it was only an act." - *noun*

*The verb '**behave**' [bee-HAYV] means 'to act or react in a specific way'. When we behave in normal ways, we usually get what we want. When we behave in ways that are not normal, it becomes more difficult to get good results.*

fake = *to behave in a way that is not a person's true feeling, or not a true story.*
"He wanted to fake that he had a gun so he could steal money from the shop."
"My sister faked [faykd] that there was a snake under my bed."
"The football player is faking that he was kicked by the other player."
"This is not a real diamond. It is a fake." - noun

cheat [cheet] = *to intend to deceive someone and take their money or their things.*
"The shopkeeper tried to cheat me. He didn't give me enough money back."
"Our business was cheated [CHEE-ted] by our customer. She never paid her bill."
"The electric company is cheating me. I did not use much electricity last month."
"The salesman was a cheat." - *noun*

steal = *to take something that belongs to another person.*
"That man tried to steal my motorcycle!"
"He stole a car, and then he stole a boat." - *past-tense changes form*
"Those girls keep stealing the flowers from my garden!"
"The police found him with the stolen money." - *adjective*
-there is no noun for 'steal'

Words for people that steal: **thief, robber, mugger, burglar, shoplifter, pickpocket, embezzler, bandit, swindler.**
All of these are **'thieves'**, but the other names are specific to the action of the crime.

mislead [miss-LEED] = *to deceive someone, or to be deceived by someone.*
"He wanted to mislead the police about where he was last night."
"I was misled [miss-LED] by the story that he was a famous actor." - *past-tense verb -*
the pronunciation changes!
"The news is misleading the people about what really happened."
"I heard a misleading story about my boss." - *adjective*

fool = *to intend to deceive someone, or to be deceived by someone.*
"She tried to fool me with her rubber snake."
"The movie fooled [foold] everyone with the surprise ending."
"You are fooling yourself if you believe your own crazy story."
"He made a fool out of me when he pushed me into the lake." - *noun*

misinform [miss-in-FORM] = *to give, or receive, information that is not correct. The information might or might not be intended to deceive someone.*
"I am not sure about the answer to your question, and I don't want to misinform you."
"The staff at the airport misinformed [miss-in-FORMD] me about when the flight would arrive."
"I don't trust the internet. There is a lot of misinformation about the news in Asia. - *noun*

Verbs to use to make events or actions stop.

surrender [sur-REND-er] = *to stop fighting and say that your side is the loser.*
"The rebel army will never surrender. They will die before they stop fighting."
"Japan surrendered [sur-REND-erd] to America in 1945."
"The boxer said 'surrendering is not my style' after he won the boxing match."

"Both armies will battle until one army's eventual surrender." - *noun*

Other phrases for 'surrender': **give up, give in, admit defeat, raise the white flag, back down, throw in the towel.**

relent [ree-LENT] = *to stop fighting or playing a game because you know that you will lose. Or, to stop because you cannot fight or play anymore. You give the 'win' to the other side.*
"I will relent the game when I become too tired to play."
"When the had no more food, the soldiers relented [ree-LEN-ted] to the enemy army."
"He will be relenting the chess match soon, because he has to return to his home."
- *no noun for 'relent'*

concede [kon-SEED] = *to stop fighting, arguing, or playing a game, because you know that you will lose. Or, to stop because you cannot fight, argue or play anymore. You give the 'win' to the other side.*
"I will have to concede the game. My wife called, and I need to go now."
"She conceded [kon-SEE-ded] that my story was correct, and her story was wrong."
"The football team is conceding the game because they do not have enough players."
-*no noun or adjective for 'concede'*
Other words and phrases for 'relent' and 'concede': **relinquish, cede** [seed]**, yield, accept defeat, back down, give up, give in, throw in the towel.**

admit [ad-MIT] = *to say the truth, or to say that you did something bad.*
"I admit it. You were right and I was wrong!"
"The boy admitted [ad-MIT-ted] that he broke the table."
"As she was admitting her love for him, he kissed her on the lips."
"The police were sure that he was the criminal after his admission of the crime." - *noun*

confess [kon-FESS] = *to say the truth, or to say that you did something bad.*
"If you do something bad, you should confess to someone."
"I didn't know that she cheated on the test until she confessed [kon-FEST] to me."
"The girl is confessing to her mother that she ate all the cake."
"The police are waiting for his confession." - *noun*

*Exercise: Make two sentences with either '**admit**' or '**confess**'. Make one sentence using past tense and one sentence using future tense.*

quit [kwit] = *to stop playing, fighting or working.*
"I am not ready to quit yet. Let's keep playing!"
"He quit his job because he did not like it." - *past-tense does not change form*
"She will be quitting school because she can't afford the cost."
- *the only noun for 'quit' is 'quitter' = someone that quits*

capitulate [kah-PIT-choo-late] = *to surrender.*
"The smaller army will capitulate to the bigger army."
"After losing his queen, he capitulated [kah-PIT-choo-late-ed] the chess game."
"Because we are tired, we are capitulating the baseball game. The other team is the winner."
- *no common noun for 'capitulate'*

submit [sub-MIT] = *to surrender, or stop trying, because of a stronger power.*
"I hope that we will not have to submit to the enemy."
"The German military submitted [sub-MIH-ted] to the Allied armies on the 8th of May, 1945."
"The horse is submitting to the horse trainer's commands."
"The German army's submission [sub-MISH-un] ended World War 2 in Europe." - *noun*

Other phrases for 'quit', 'capitulate' and 'submit': **give up, give in, raise the white flag, back down, throw in the towel, yield to.**

These are not the only definitions for many of these words. The lessons in this book are intended to teach usage for specific categories of ideas and concepts.
*We hope that your skills will improve using **English Everyday**.*

One more important verb to know is:

succeed [suk-SEED], which means *'to reach your goal'*

"You will **succeed** if you do not quit!"

This is OUR goal at **English Everyday**. We want you to succeed with **your** goal of learning English. It is not always easy, but *YOU CAN DO IT!*

Please look at our videos on YouTube for pronunciation.
*Listen, learn and practice! Find the link at **EnglishEveryday.info***

---

*To '**retain**' information means 'to keep it in your memory'.*
Now that you have studied the words, practiced the pronunciation,
completed the exercises, and are familiar with many new words
*and phrases, it is time to test your '**retention**'. How much have you*
remembered?

These are words from the book. Most of the words are verbs, plus a few phrases.

Try your best, and test yourself to see what you have **retained**.

Some of the questions have more than one correct answer!

If something **collides**, does it

1. hit another thing?
2. make something longer?
3. fall down?
4. try to break another thing?

Why would someone **duck down**?

1. To try a new dance style.
2. Because the room is too small.
3. To avoid hitting their head.
4. To put shoes on their feet.

What is the definition of **crush**?

1. Make a loud sound.
2. Make something smaller by using force.
3. Make a circle shape with a long rope.
4. Destroy something so it does not work anymore.

What does **able** mean?

1. Strong and healthy.
2. Beautiful and popular.
3. Can understand something.
4. Can do something.

What does the noun **category** mean?

1. All the parts of something.
2. Things in a group that are similar.
3. Many people in a group.
4. Things in a group that are different.

What does the adjective **specific** mean?

1. Anything in a category.
2. Many things in a group of things.
3. One thing in a group of things.
4. One thing that is similar to another thing.

Choose the definition of the verb **to picture**.

1. Imagine something that you cannot see.
2. Use a pencil and paper to make a picture.
3. Make a photo.
4. Remember a dream.

If I **provoke** somebody, I am

1. trying to make the person return to their home.
2. agreeing with their opinion.
3. trying to make the person sad.
4. intending to make that person angry.

When I **grab** something, I

1. use my body to move it to a different place.
2. touch it with all the fingers of one hand.
3. use my hand to pick it up quickly.
4. hit it with my hand.

If I **"give up"**, that means that I

1. give something to someone.
2. stop trying.
3. look at the clouds.
4. move my hands above my head.

Why would I **squint** my eyes?

1. To communicate with someone without words.
2. Because I have dirt in my eyes.
3. The light is too bright.
4. Because I want to be beautiful.

What am I doing if I am **humming**?

1. Making a table or a chair using electric tools.
2. Working very quickly.
3. Saying something that is not true.
4. Making the sounds of a song without singing.

Why would I **tremble**?

1. Because I am cold or scared.
2. Because I am excited and happy.
3. Because my feet hurt.
4. Because I cannot stand up.

If I saw something **wrecked**, what could it be?
1. Food that is too hot.
2. A person fell down and hit their head.
3. A bottle smashed on the floor.
4. A car hit a tree.

If I want to **punch** something, I need to
1. grab it and shake it.
2. hit it with something soft.
3. hit it with my fist.
4. be very angry.

How do you say **advise**?
1. AD-vize
2. ad-VIZE
3. ad-VICE
4. ad-VEEZ

If you say to your mother "I am going to study English", but you do not study, you look at Facebook instead. What did you do to your mother?
1. Deceive her.
2. Confess to her.
3. Mislead her.
4. Anticipate her.

Which is the correct form of the verb in each sentence?
1. Did you _____ what I said to you yesterday? • heard • hearing • hear
2. My arm did not _____ very good this morning. • felt • feel • feeled
3. I went to the shop and _____ a new shirt. • buy • bought • buying
4. She walks to school instead of _____ to school. • run • running • runs
5. I understood everything that you _____ to me. • said • sayed • say
6. We will _____ these three things. • combining • combine • combination
7. I can't _____ the taste of onions! • wait • stand • eat • smell
8. The tree is _____ the view of the sky. • obscure • obscured • obscuring

Which is the correct phonetic pronunciation of **cough**?
1. kaw   2. kofe   3. koff   4. kowf

Which words are similar to the word **combine**?
1. mix   2. stir   3. chop   4. blend

A bomb will not **explode** until it is
1. incited   2. toppled   3. detonated   4. provoked

What is the best word to describe how the moon moves around the earth?
1. It **spins** around the earth 2. It **rotates** around the earth 3. It **twirls** around the earth

Use the best **helping verbs** for these sentences.
There might be more than one correct answer!
"We _____ go to the beach today."
"We _____ going to the beach today, but we are not sure."
"Yesterday, she _____ thinking about her friend. Today, she _____ visiting her friend."
"The wheel _____ spinning, but now it _____ stopped spinning."
"If I _____ wanted to go with you, I _____ gone with you."
"We _____ eating at 6 o'clock this evening."
"We _____ eat at 6 o'clock this evening."
"Later today, they _____ going to the market, depending on if it _____ raining."
"We have no food! We _____ go to the market."
"We _____ going to the market now."
"When the weather is very cold, you _____ wear a jacket."
"The weather is cold, and he _____ wearing a jacket."
"He _____ have a car, but now he does not."
"Sorry, I _____ go with you today, but tomorrow I _____ go with you."
"Later today, we _____ visiting our grandmother."
"We _____ visiting our grandmother now."

Answers to the test:

If something **collides**, does it
1. hit another thing? **correct**
2. make something longer?
3. fall down?
4. try to break another thing?

Why would someone **duck down**?
1. To try a new dance style.
2. Because the room is too small.
3. To avoid hitting their head. **correct**
4. To put shoes on their feet.

What is the definition of **crush**?
1. Make a loud sound.
2. Make something smaller by using force. **correct**
3. Make a circle shape with a long rope.
4. Destroy something so it does not work anymore. **possibly correct**

What does **able** mean?
1. Strong and healthy.
2. Beautiful and popular.
3. Can understand something.
4. Can do something. **correct**

What does the noun **category** mean?
1. All the parts of something.
2. Things in a group that are similar. **correct**
3. Many people in a group.
4. Things in a group that are different.

What does the adjective **specific** mean?
1. Anything in a category.
2. Many things in a group of things.
3. One thing in a group of things. **correct**
4. One thing that is similar to another thing.

Choose the definition of the verb **to picture**.

1. Imagine something that you cannot see. **correct**
2. Use a pencil and paper to make a picture.
3. Make a photo.
4. Remember a dream.

If I **provoke** somebody, I am

1. trying to make the person return to their home.
2. agreeing with their opinion.
3. trying to make the person sad.
4. intending to make that person angry. **correct**

When I **grab** something, I

1. use my body to move it to a different place.
2. touch it with all the fingers of one hand.
3. use my hand to pick it up quickly. **correct**
4. hit it with my hand.

If I **"give up"**, that means that I

1. give something to someone.
2. stop trying. **correct**
3. look at the clouds.
4. move my hands above my head.

Why would I **squint** my eyes?

1. To communicate with someone without words.
2. Because I have dirt in my eyes.
3. The light is too bright. **correct**
4. Because I want to be beautiful.

What am I doing if I am **humming**?

1. Making a table or a chair using electric tools.
2. Working very quickly.
3. Saying something that is not true.
4. Making the sounds of a song without singing. **correct**

Why would I **tremble**?

1. Because I am cold or scared. **correct**
2. Because I am excited and happy.
3. Because my feet hurt.
4. Because I cannot stand up.

If I saw something **wrecked**, what could it be?

1. Food that is too hot.
2. A person fell down and hit their head.
3. A bottle smashed on the floor.
4. A car hit a tree. **correct**

If I want to **punch** something, I need to

1. grab it and shake it.
2. hit it with something soft.
3. hit it with my fist. **correct**
4. be very angry.

How do you say **advise**?

1. AD-vize
2. ad-VIZE **correct**
3. ad-VICE
4. ad-VEEZ

If you say to your mother "I am going to study English", but you do not study. You look at Facebook instead. What did you do to your mother?

1. Deceive her. **correct**
2. Confess to her.
3. Mislead her. **correct**
4. Anticipate her.

Which is the correct form of the verb in each sentence?
1. Did you _____ what I said to you yesterday? • heard • hearing • **hear**
2. My arm did not _____ very good this morning. • felt • **feel** • feeled
3. I went to the shop and _____ a new shirt. • buy • **bought** • buying
4. She walks to school instead of _____ to school. • run • **running** • runs
5. I understood everything that you _____ to me. • **said** • sayed • say
6. We will _____ these three things. • combining • **combine** • combination
7. I can't _____ the taste of onions! • wait • **stand** • eat • smell
8. The tree is _____ the view of the sky. • obscure • obscured • **obscuring**

Which is the correct phonetic pronunciation of **cough**?
1. kaw   2. kofe   **3. koff**   4. kowf

Which words are similar to the word **combine**?
1. mix   2. stir   3. chop   **4. blend**

A bomb will not **explode** until it is
1. incited   2. toppled   **3. detonated**   4. provoked

What is the best word to describe how the moon moves around the earth?
1. It spins around the earth **2. It rotates around the earth** 3. It twirls around the earth

Use the best **helping verbs** for these sentences.
There might be more than one correct answer!
"We **will** *or* **shall** go to the beach today."
"We **might be** *or* **may be** going to the beach today, but we are not sure."
"Yesterday, she **was** thinking about her friend. Today, she **is** *or* **will be** visiting her friend."
"The wheel **was** spinning, but now it **has** stopped spinning."
"If I **had** wanted to go with you, I **would have** gone with you."
"We **will be** *or* **shall be** eating at 6 o'clock this evening."
"We **will** *or* **shall** eat at 6 o'clock this evening."
"Later today, they **are** *or* **will be** going to the market, depending on if it **is** *or* **will be** raining."
"We have no food! We **should, have to** *or* **must** go to the market."
"We **are** *or* **will be** going to the market now."
"When the weather is very cold, you **should, can** *or* **must** wear a jacket."

91

"The weather is cold, and he **is** wearing a jacket."

"He **used to** have a car, but now he does not."

"Sorry, I **can't** go with you today, but tomorrow I **can** go with you."

"Later today, we **will be** visiting our grandmother."

"We **are** visiting our grandmother now."

INDEX

perception 46, 47, 48, 78

permit 61

perpetually 71

persevere 72, 73

persistently 71

picture 55, 84, 89

pledge 68

plow into 38

plug away 72

polish 30

ponder 51

pour 17

prerequisite 64

press ahead 72

press on 72

presume 51

pretend 66, 67

proceed 71, 72, 73

prod 70

progress 71, 72, 73

promise 67, 68

pronouncing the 'TH' sounds
 1

provoke 70, 85, 89

pull 2, 24, 41

pull apart 41

pull down 41

punch 38, 86, 90

pungent 47

punish 73

push 24, 29

put up with 74

Q

quit 59, 72, 82, 83

quiver 22

R

racket 48

raise the white flag 81, 82

ramble 4

rattle on 4

raze 28

reach the goal 68

reason 54, 56, 73

reckon 56

recognize 2, 13, 64, 76, 78

recommend 65, 69

reeking 47

reflect iv, 58

regard 58

relent 81

relinquish 81

remove all traces of 43

repeatedly 71

require 64

resemble 76

result 14, 19, 23, 36, 38, 48, 50, 55, 56,
 65, 72, 73, 79

retain 83

return on investment 73

revolve 18, 19

reward 72, 73

roll around 19

rotate 18, 19, 87, 91

rough estimate 57

rough estimation 57

rub 1, 30

ruin 40

run into 38

run on and on about 4

run the numbers 58

S

saw 6, 11, 12, 21, 23, 30, 40, 43, 44, 52, 75, 78, 86, 90

say it out loud 10, 13, 41, 57

scent 47

scented 47

scrape 26, 27

scratch 27

scream 5, 74

screen v, 32

scrub 30

scrutinize 59

seem 48, 70

see the difference between 77

separate the pieces 41

sequester 33

serpentine 20

set apart 77

set aside 68

set your sights on 62

sever 44

shake 21, 23, 65, 86, 90

shall 26, 91

shatter 45

shed 13

shiver 22

a shot in the arm 69

should 2, 7, 10, 20, 26, 34, 54, 56, 58, 65, 69, 81, 91

shout 5

shroud 33

shuffle 9

shut down 41

sigh 12

sing 15, 60, 61

six feet under 35

slam into 38

slap 15, 38, 39

slice 17

smack 38, 39

smack into 38

smash 27, 28, 38, 44

smash into 38

smell 17, 34, 46, 47, 53, 74, 86, 91

snap 15, 35, 37

snapped off 46

snap your fingers 15

snatch 5, 6

sneak 10

a sneaking suspicion 48

sneeze 12, 47

sound v, 1, 3, 4, 10, 11, 12, 15, 20, 22, 23, 35, 36, 37, 39, 44, 45, 47, 48, 49, 50, 59, 60, 78, 84, 85, 88, 89

spark off 70

spasm 12, 22, 23

speak favorably about 69

speaking to yourself 4

speak under your breath 4

speak well of 69

specific 25, 47, 60, 63, 64, 75, 78, 79, 80, 82, 84, 88

specify 77, 78

spin 18, 19, 20, 87, 91

spiral 19, 20

splinter 45

spot 30, 75

spur on 69, 70

squeeze 27, 30

squint 13, 85, 89

squirm 21

stand 8, 32, 72, 74, 85, 86, 90, 91

stand up straight 8

stand your ground 72

Y

Printed in the United States
By Bookmasters